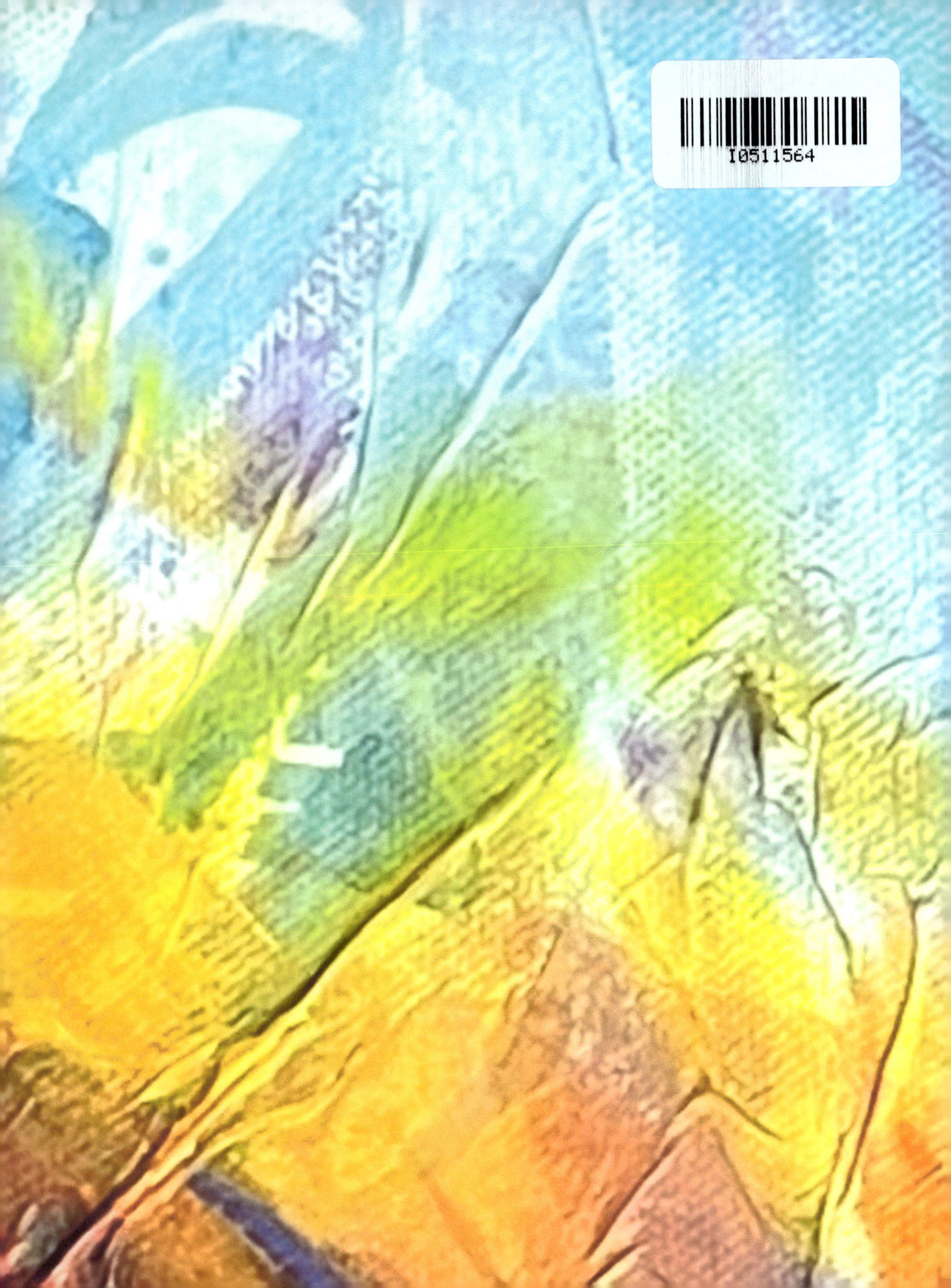

Into the Lion's Mane

Painted Psalms of Comfort and Hope

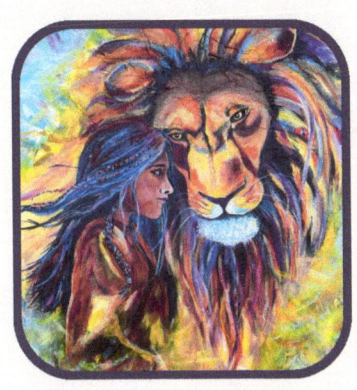

Compiled and Illustrated by
Starla D. Henninger

This book addresses some of the feelings and prayers one might experience going through grief. It's a compilation of Scripture and artwork with the artist's notes in the back.

Copyright © 2025 by Artist and Author, Starla D. Henninger.
All rights reserved. No portion of this book may be reproduced, distributed, or transmitted in any form without prior written permission from the author, except as permitted by U.S. copyright law.
For permission requests, contact Starla Henninger at: Starla@QuietRiverCreations.com

ISBN: 979-8-218-86257-2.

Scripture quotations taken from the Amplified® Bible (AMP), Copyright © 2015 by The Lockman Foundation. Used by permission. lockman.org

Scripture quotations marked CSB have been taken from the Christian Standard Bible®, Copyright © 2017 by Holman Bible Publishers. Used by permission. Christian Standard Bible® and CSB® are federally registered trademarks of Holman Bible Publishers.

Taken from the Complete Jewish Bible by David H. Stern. Copyright © 1998. All rights reserved. Used by permission of Messianic Jewish Publishers, 6120 Day Long Lane, Clarksville, MD 21029. messianicjewish.net.

Holy Bible: Easy-to-Read Version™
Taken from the HOLY BIBLE: EASY-TO-READ VERSION™
© 2006 by Bible League International and used by permission.

Scripture quotations taken from the (NASB®) New American Standard Bible®, Copyright © 2020 by The Lockman Foundation. Used by permission. All rights reserved.
lockman.org

Scripture quotations marked (NLT) are taken from the Holy Bible, New Living Translation, copyright ©1996, 2004, 2015 by Tyndale House Foundation. Used by permission of Tyndale House Publishers, Carol Stream, Illinois 60188. All rights reserved.

Scripture quotations marked NLV are taken from the New Life Version, Copyright © 1969 and 2003. Used by permission of Barbour Publishing, Inc., Uhrichsville, Ohio 44683. All rights reserved.

The following abbreviations are used:
Amplified Bible (AMP)
Christian Standard Bible (CSB)
The Complete Jewish Bible (CJB)
Easy-to-Read Version (ERV)
New American Standard Bible (NASB)
New Living Translation (NLT)
New Life Version (NLV)

In loving memory of
two amazing fathers bookending this project.

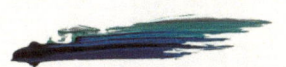

Sharing excitement about the vision of this book,
my dear late father-in-law,
Thomas Henninger Sr.,
at this moment beholds our Savior's face.
His contagious laughter now
fills heaven's ears.

Cheering encouragement up to this finalization,
my own sweet father,
Eldon Shetler,
presently is in the presence of Christ.
His soothing bass voice now
resonates with that heavenly throng.

All praise and glory goes to the
Author of creativity,
to the Giver of abilities;
my Lord and Savior,
Jesus Christ!

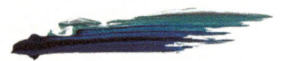

Attempting to name
the numerous people who have
been a vital part of this journey is impossible.
A heart-felt thank you for your
encouragement, support, input, and care!

Contents

Introduction 1

Help Me, God 5

I need You 21

Be Still, My Heart 33

The Savior is Near 45

His Plans are Good 57

Artist's Notes 71

How Can I Know Jesus? 80

About the Artist 85

Dear Friend,

Pain. Suffering. Heartache. Loss. All are part of the human experience. No one is exempt. Sometimes life hits us out of nowhere and leaves us bewildered and shocked. Even years later, loss, neglect, abuse, loneliness, or rejection, often is felt all over again. We are broken people.

One of God's names is "El-Roi", meaning

"The God who sees"

In Genesis 16:13, Hagar, an Egyptian slave who was abused and rejected came to the stunning realization that God saw her. Even in the middle of the desert, with her dying son being the only other soul around, God saw. The Amplified Version emphasizes that He saw her with understanding and compassion. The God who still sees is deeply aware of you and your situation. The One who crafted you while still in the womb, knows you like no one else.

This book is filled with paintings and verses primarily from the book of Psalms. (Some tied-in cross references are added to give deeper meaning as observed in other Scriptures) The Psalmist paves the way in pouring out his raw emotions and feelings to God. There is no shame in that. There are the "Why God?" moments, the times where he pours out his sorrow to God, and also times where he realizes that God is the only One who can be fully trusted through gut wrenching grief.

On these pages, strong emotions are not hiding. They are a part of our experiences as we walk through heartache. God's Word addresses our needs and Scripture is included without explanations or elaborations. I am praying that God will take His powerful sharp Word and by His Spirit speak to the depths of your spirit as only He can.

*I pour out my complaints before him
and tell him all my troubles. Psalm 142:2 (NLT)*

*"Every word of God has been proven true.
He is a safe-covering to
those who trust in Him." Proverbs 30:5 (NLV).*

You will notice that the verses are written out in a number of different translations. Some are easier to understand than others. For the person who is a new Christian or hasn't had a background in church, the *King James Version* can be difficult to understand. Two translations that put Scripture in a very child-like way so as to make it simple to understand are the *New Life Version* and the *Easy-to-Read Version*.

The *New Life Version* was originally written for those whose first language is not English. The vocabulary is limited. The *Easy-to-Read Version* was originally translated for the deaf community. It is also very easy to read, hence the name. In exploring verses in these two translations, it was like seeing God's Word through the eyes of a child again, and I hope they can be refreshing to you, too.

This is meant to be read like a devotional; just a page or two daily. **The main Scripture written in bold is what the painting is attempting to illustrate in some way.** The verses underneath in lighter font are cross references to go along with the main Scripture.

Jesus often illustrated truth via word pictures. It is said that a picture is worth a thousand words. In the traditional sense of writing many pages of material, I am not an author, but God has put a paintbrush in my hand and through the strokes of a brush He communicates truth. These paintings are created by using various art mediums to express the ideas that have come to mind while thinking and praying about the verse(s).

At the back, you will find thumbnail versions of each painting with a short description. You may find it helpful to reference these while you go through the pages.

I pray the Holy Spirit will use these paintings and His living Word, to speak to your life in a fresh way. He alone is the Healer of broken hearts. He alone is the Master Mender. He is the only true Savior, the loving Shepherd, the Lion of Judah and returning King. He still invites us to draw near to Him because He is the God who sees.

In the beauty of His presence, sorrow is dimmed. Under the Refuge of His mane, storms can be faced. May your heart experience peace and strength as He enfolds you in His loving and powerful presence.
His invitation is for all who are weary and heavy laden to come to Him. Step into the Lion's mane, and He will give you rest.

By His grace,

Starla

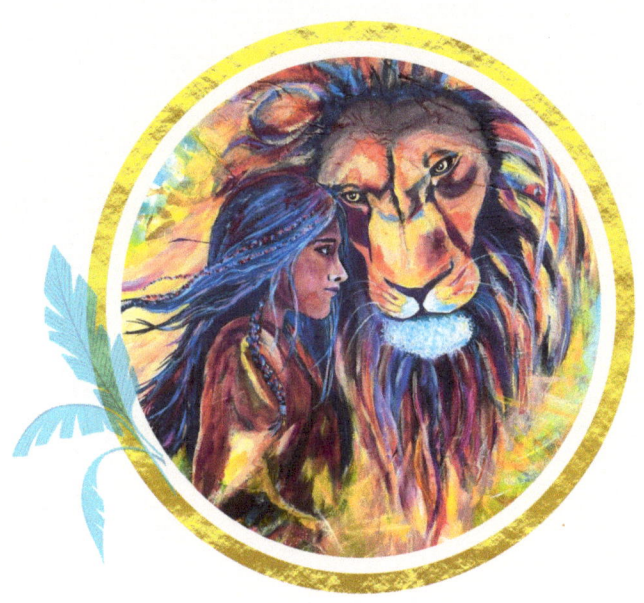

Help Me, God!

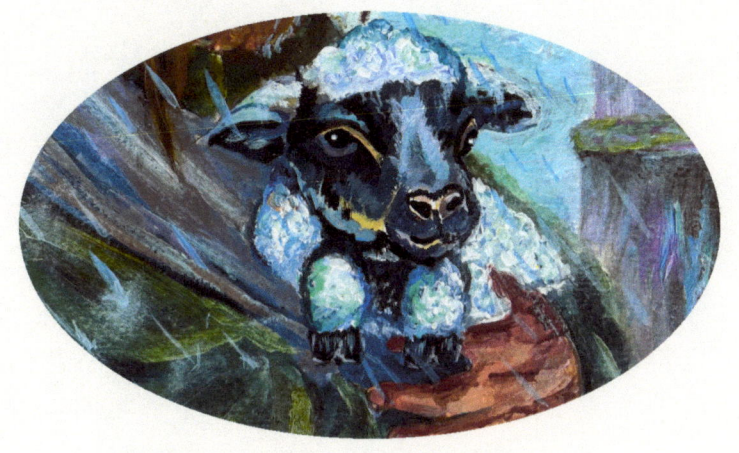

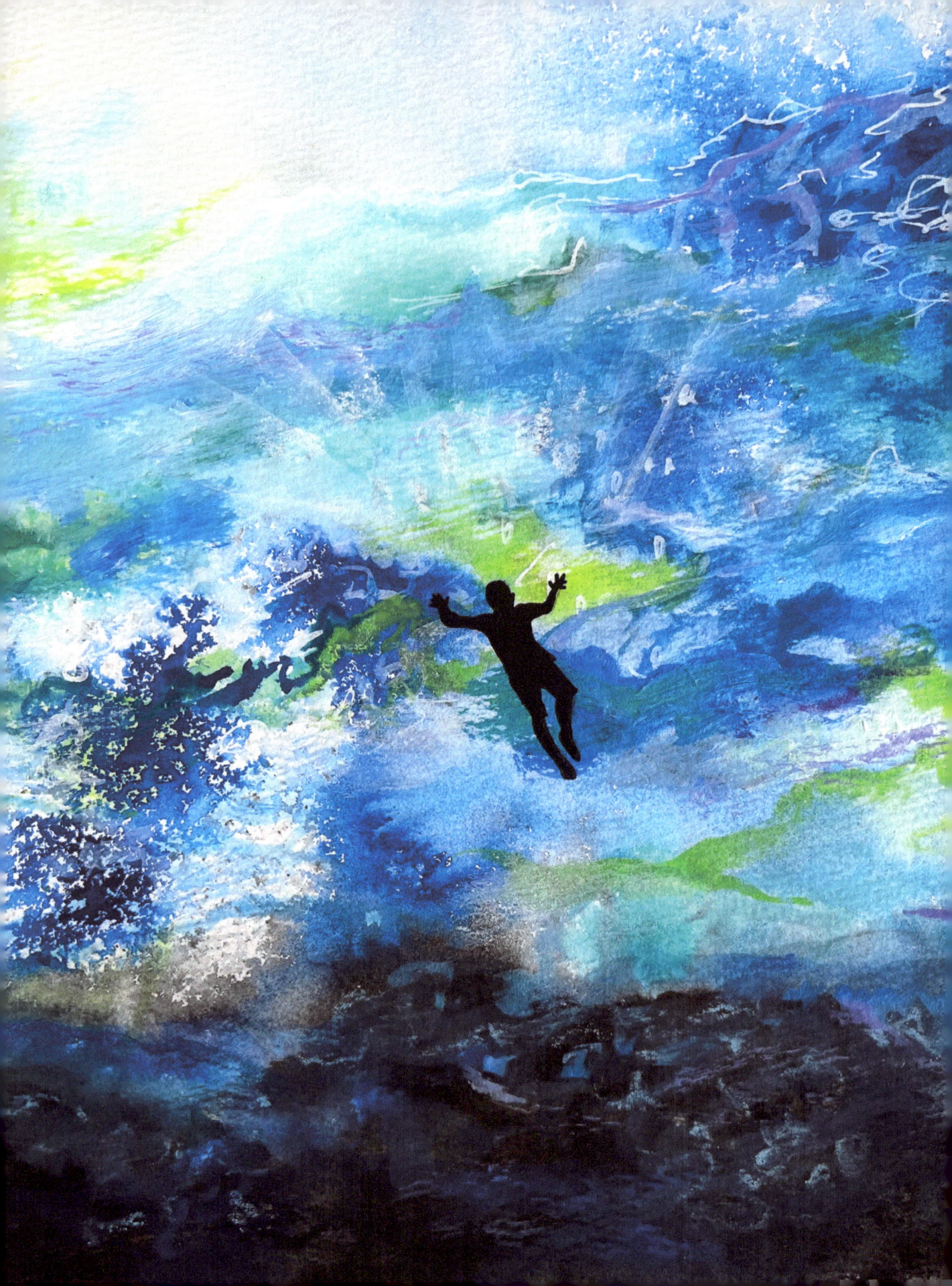

Psalm 69:1-3 (AMP)

**Save me, O God,
for the waters have come up
to my neck [they threaten my life].**

**I sink in deep mire, where there is no foothold;
I have come into deep waters,
where the floods overwhelm me.**

**I am weary with my crying;
my throat is parched;
my eyes fail with waiting [hopefully] for my God.**

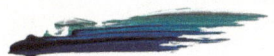

You threw me into the ocean depths,
and I sank down
to the heart of the sea.
The mighty waters engulfed me;
I was buried beneath your wild and stormy waves..
Jonah 2:3 (NLT)

My God, I kept calling by day,
and I was not silent at night.
But you did not answer me. Psalm 22:2 (ERV)

My eyes grow weary
looking for what you have promised;
I ask, "When will you comfort me?" Psalm 119:82 (CSB)

Lord, I am so weak. I cried to you all night. My pillow is soaked;
my bed is dripping wet from my tears.
Psalm 6:6 (ERV)

Psalm 69:13,15-17 (NLT)

But I keep praying
to you, Lord,
hoping this time
you will show me favor.
In your unfailing love, O God,
answer my prayer with your sure salvation.

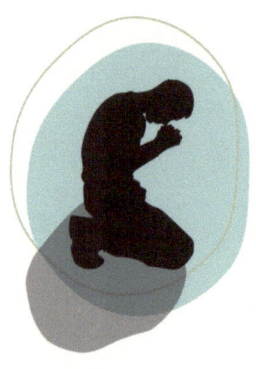

Don't let the floods overwhelm me,
or the deep waters swallow me,
or the pit of death devour me.

Answer my prayers, O Lord,
for your unfailing love is wonderful.
Take care of me, for your mercy is so plentiful.

Don't hide from your servant;
answer me quickly, for I am in deep trouble

But I call to God, and the Lord will save me.
I complain and groan morning, noon, and night,
and he hears my voice. Psalm 55:16, 17 (CSB)

Turn to me and have mercy,
for I am alone and in deep distress. Psalm 25:16 (NLT)

Don't turn away from me. Don't be angry with your servant.
You are the only one who can help me.
My God, don't leave me all alone. You are my Savior.
Psalm 27:9 (ERV)

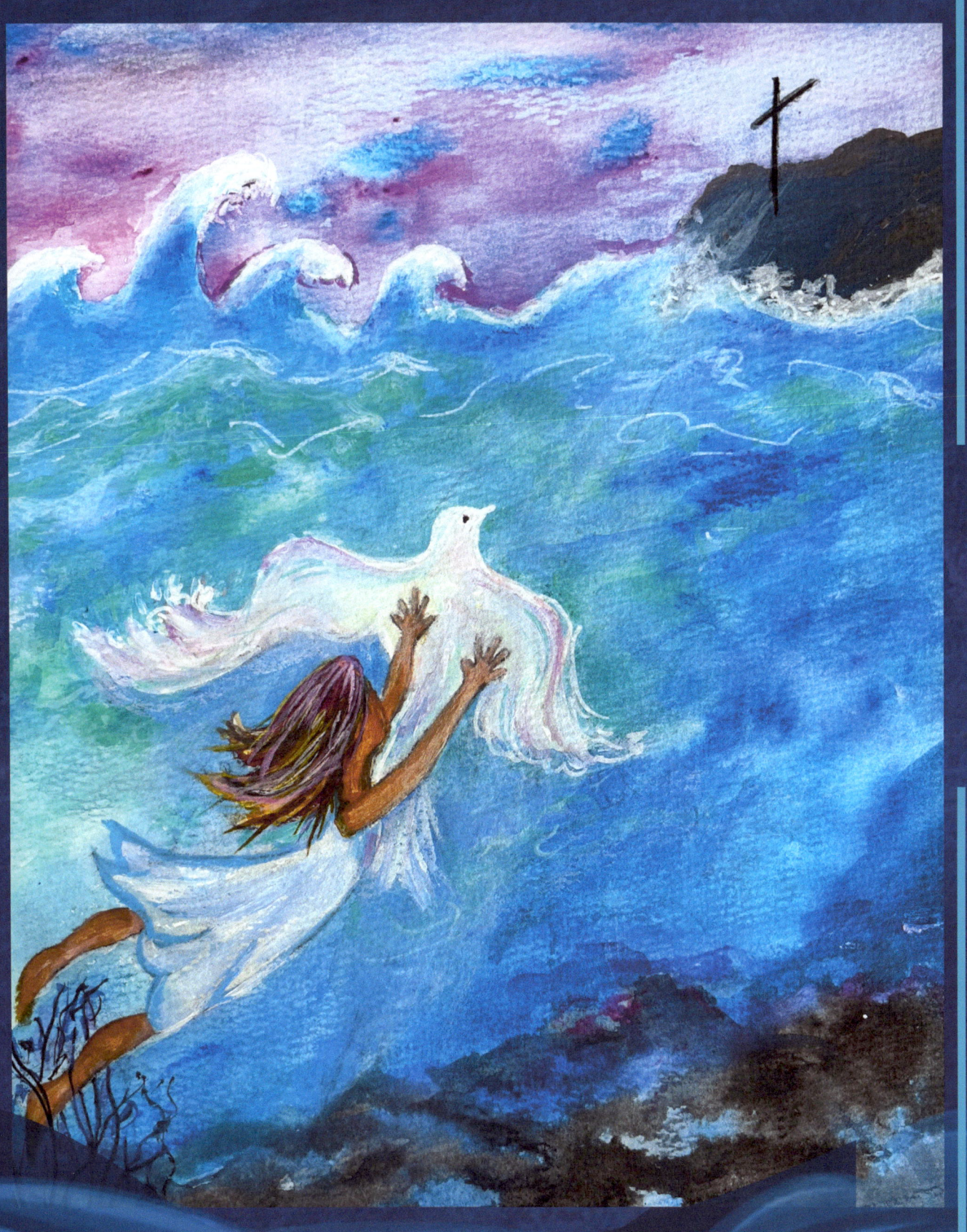

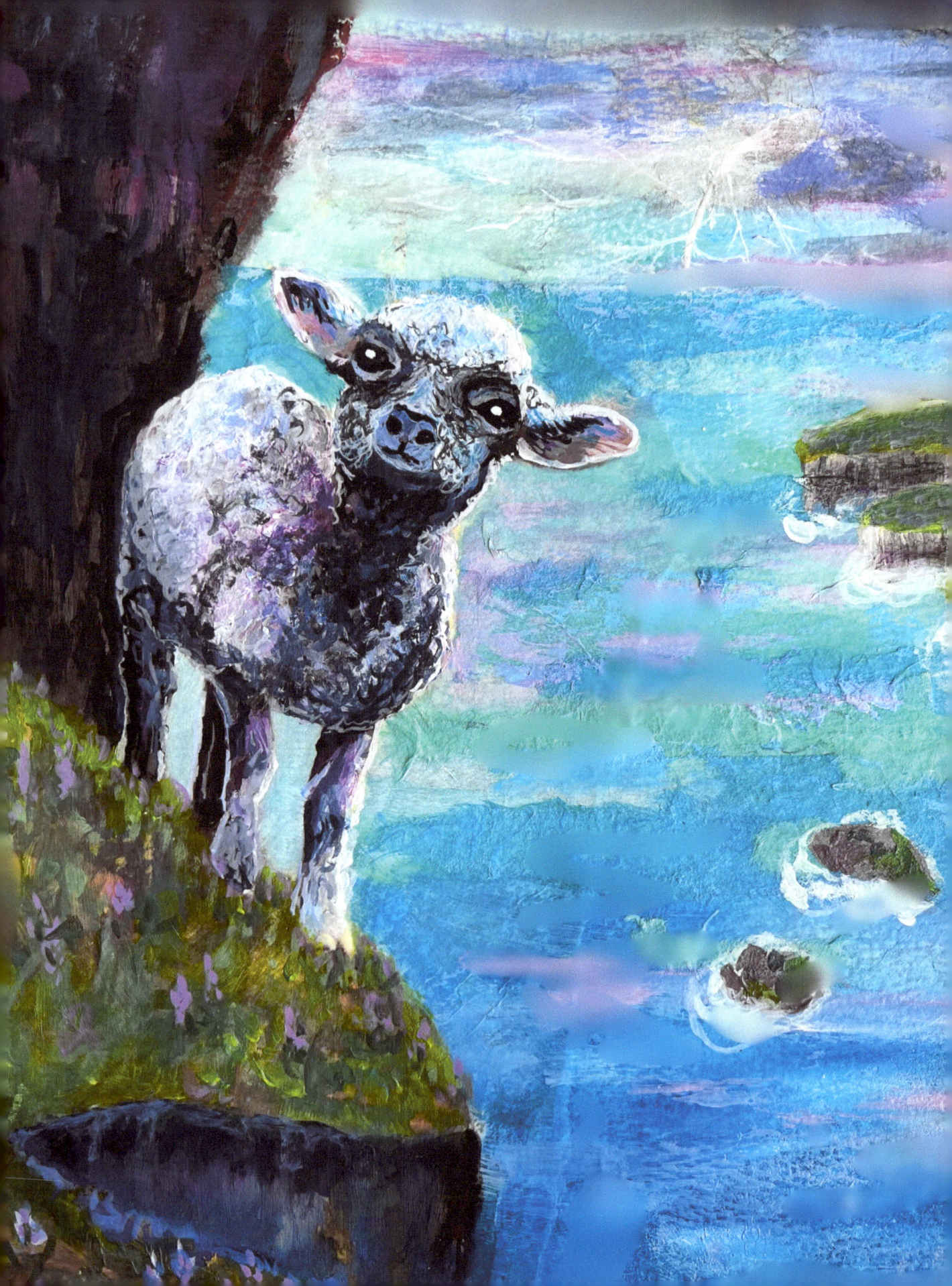

Psalm 86:1-6 (NLV)

Hear, O Lord, and answer me.
For I am suffering and in need.

Keep my life, for I am faithful to You. You are my God.
Save Your servant who trusts in You.

Show me loving-kindness, O Lord. For I cry to You all day long.

Bring joy to Your servant. For I lift up my soul to You, O Lord.

For You are good and ready to forgive, O Lord.
You are rich in loving-kindness to all who call to You.

Hear my prayer, O Lord. Listen to my cry for help.

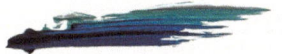

"Great blessings belong to those who know they are spiritually in need.
God's kingdom belongs to them. Matt. 5:3 (ERV)

Restore to me the joy of your salvation,
and make me willing to obey you. Psalm 51:12 (NLT)

Yes, whoever continues to ask will receive.
Whoever continues to look will find.
And whoever continues to knock
will have the door opened for them.
Luke 11:10 (ERV)

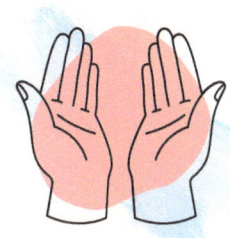

*Psalm
86:7, 11-17
(CSB)*

I call on you
in the day of my distress,
for you will answer me.

Teach me your way, Lord,
and I will live by your truth.
Give me an undivided mind to fear your name.

I will praise you with all my heart, Lord my God,
and will honor your name forever.

For your faithful love for me is great,
and you rescue my life from the depths of Sheol.

God, arrogant people have attacked me;
a gang of ruthless men intends to kill me.
They do not let you guide them.

But you, Lord, are a compassionate and gracious God,
slow to anger and abounding in faithful love and truth.

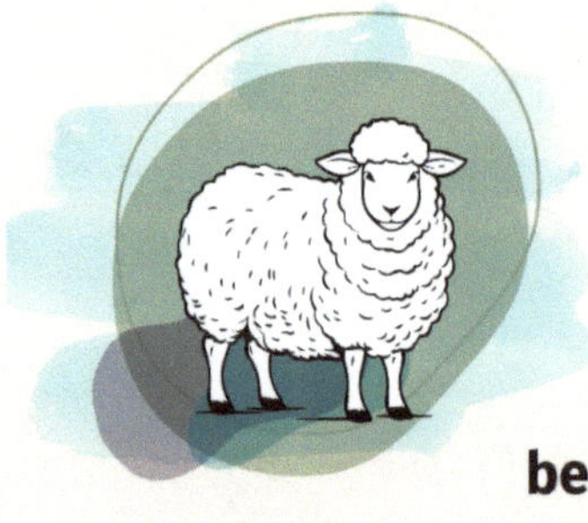

Turn to me and be gracious to me.
Give your strength to your servant;
save the son of your female servant.

Show me a sign of your goodness;
my enemies will see and be put to shame
because you, Lord, have helped and comforted me.

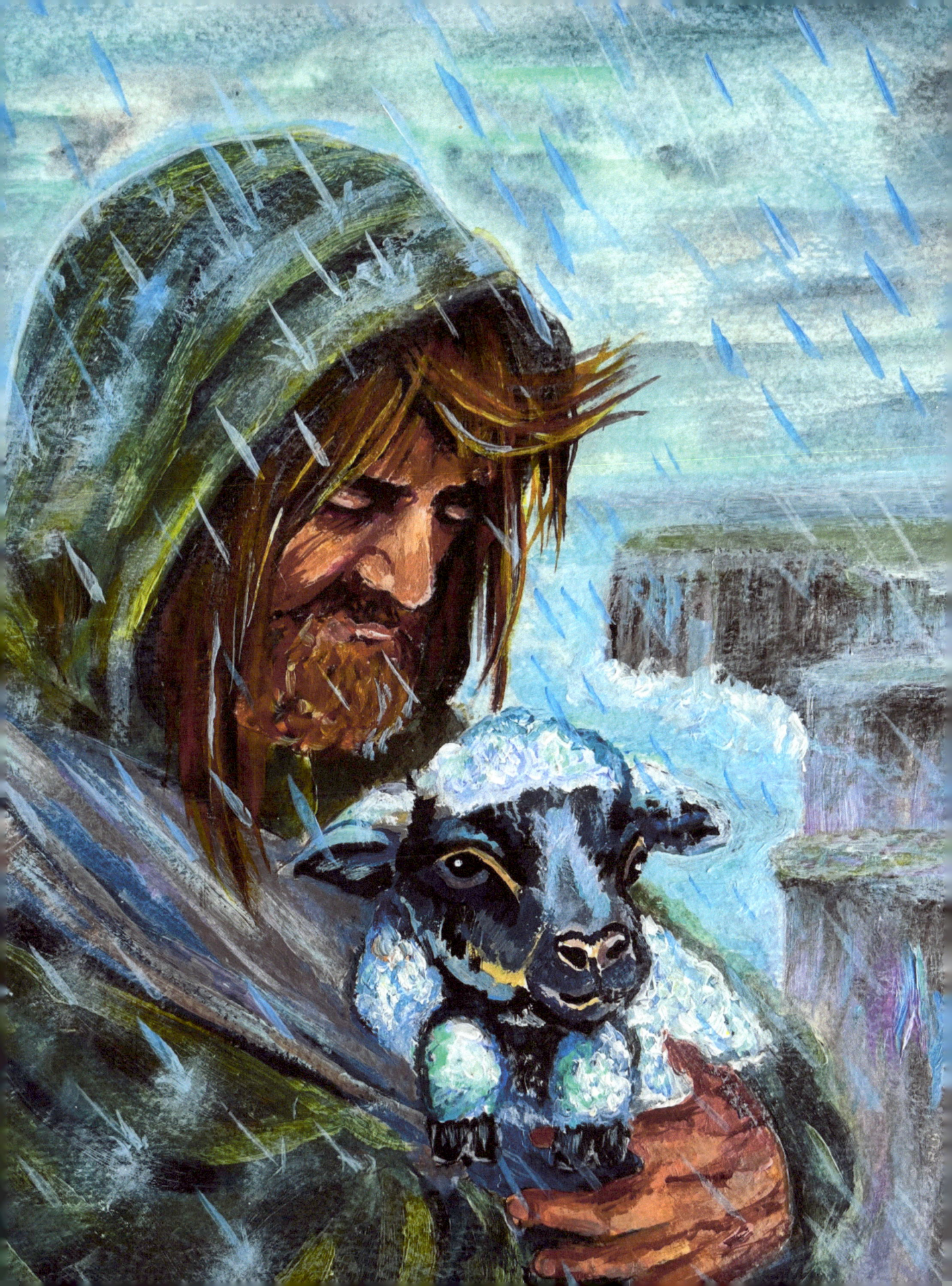

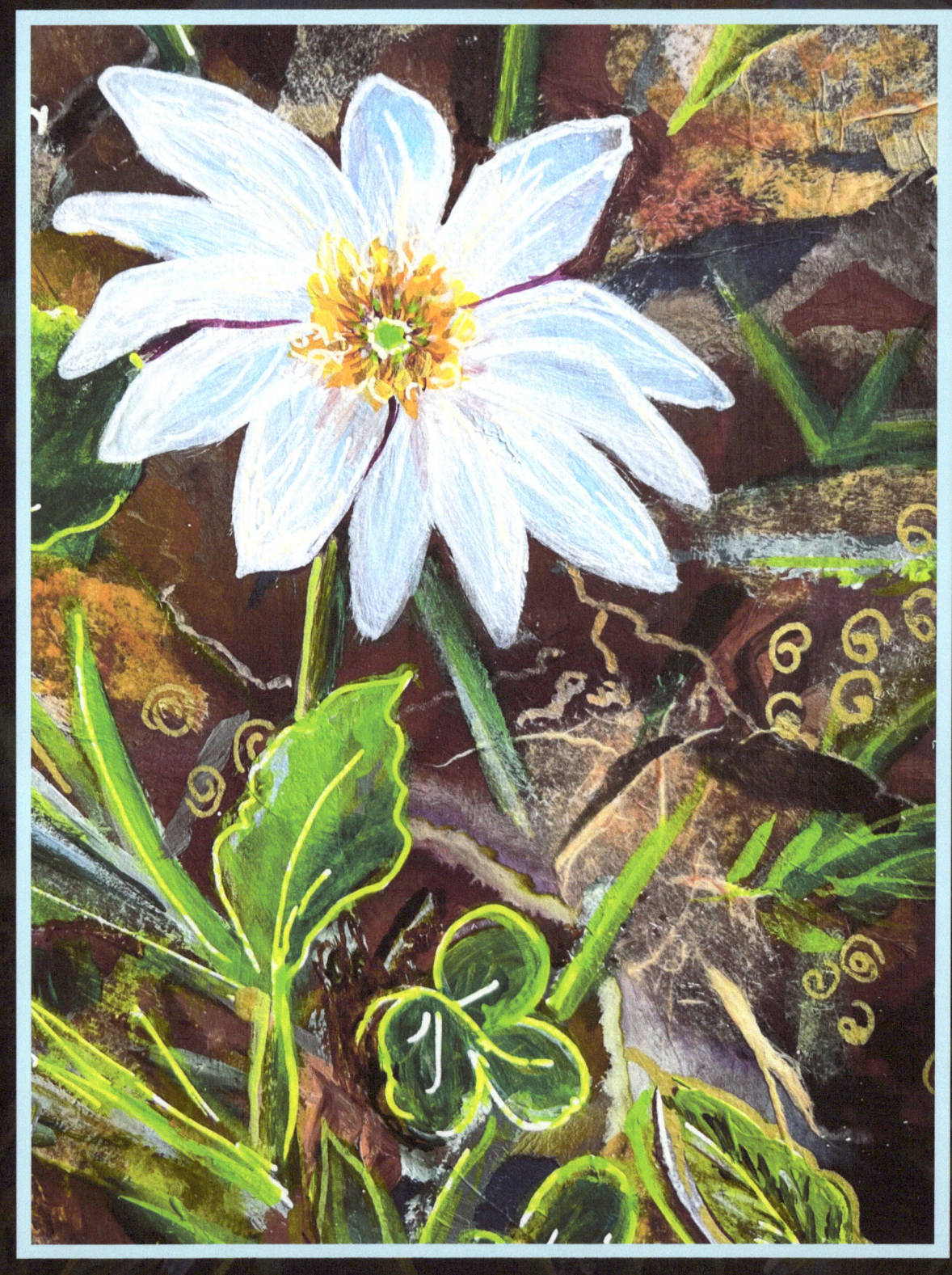

Psalm 86:11 (NLT)

**Teach me your ways, O Lord,
that I may live
according to your truth!
Grant me purity of heart,
so that I may honor you.**

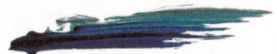

Have mercy on me, O God, because of your unfailing love.
Because of your great compassion, blot out the stain of my sins.

Wash me clean from my guilt. Purify me from my sin.
For I recognize my rebellion; it haunts me day and night.

Against you, and you alone, have I sinned;
I have done what is evil in your sight.
You will be proved right in what you say,
and your judgment against me is just.

For I was born a sinner—
yes, from the moment my mother conceived me.
But you desire honesty from the womb,
teaching me wisdom even there.

Purify me from my sins, and I will be clean;
wash me, and I will be whiter than snow.
Oh, give me back my joy again;
you have broken me— now let me rejoice.
Don't keep looking at my sins. Remove the stain of my guilt.

Create in me a clean heart, O God.
Renew a loyal spirit within me.
The sacrifice you desire is a broken spirit.
You will not reject a broken and repentant heart, O God.
Psalm 51:1-10, 17 (NLT)

Psalm 61:1-4 (AMP)

Hear my cry, O God;
Listen to my prayer.

From the end of the earth I call to You,
when my heart is overwhelmed and weak;
Lead me to the rock that is higher than I
[a rock that is too high to reach without Your help].

For You have been a shelter and a refuge for me,
A strong tower against the enemy.

Let me dwell in Your tent forever;
Let me take refuge in the shelter of Your wings. Selah.

He will protect me when I am in danger.
He will hide me in his tent.
He will take me up to his place of safety.
Psalm 27:5 (ERV)

The name of Adonai is a strong tower;
a righteous person runs to it and is raised high
[above danger].
Proverbs 18:10 (CJB)

May the Lord, the God of Israel, under whose wings you
have come to take refuge, reward you fully for what you
have done."
Ruth 2:12 (NLT)

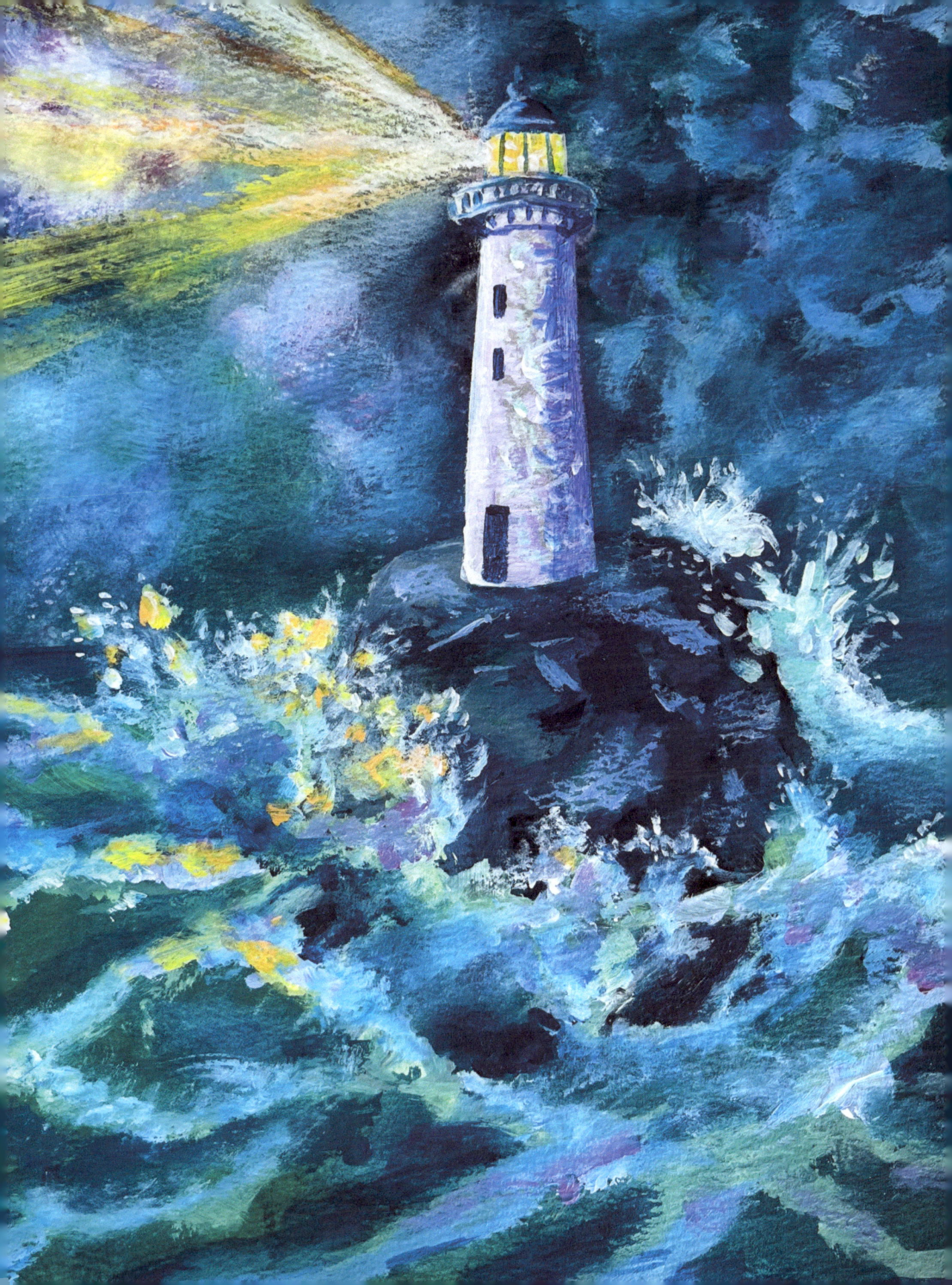

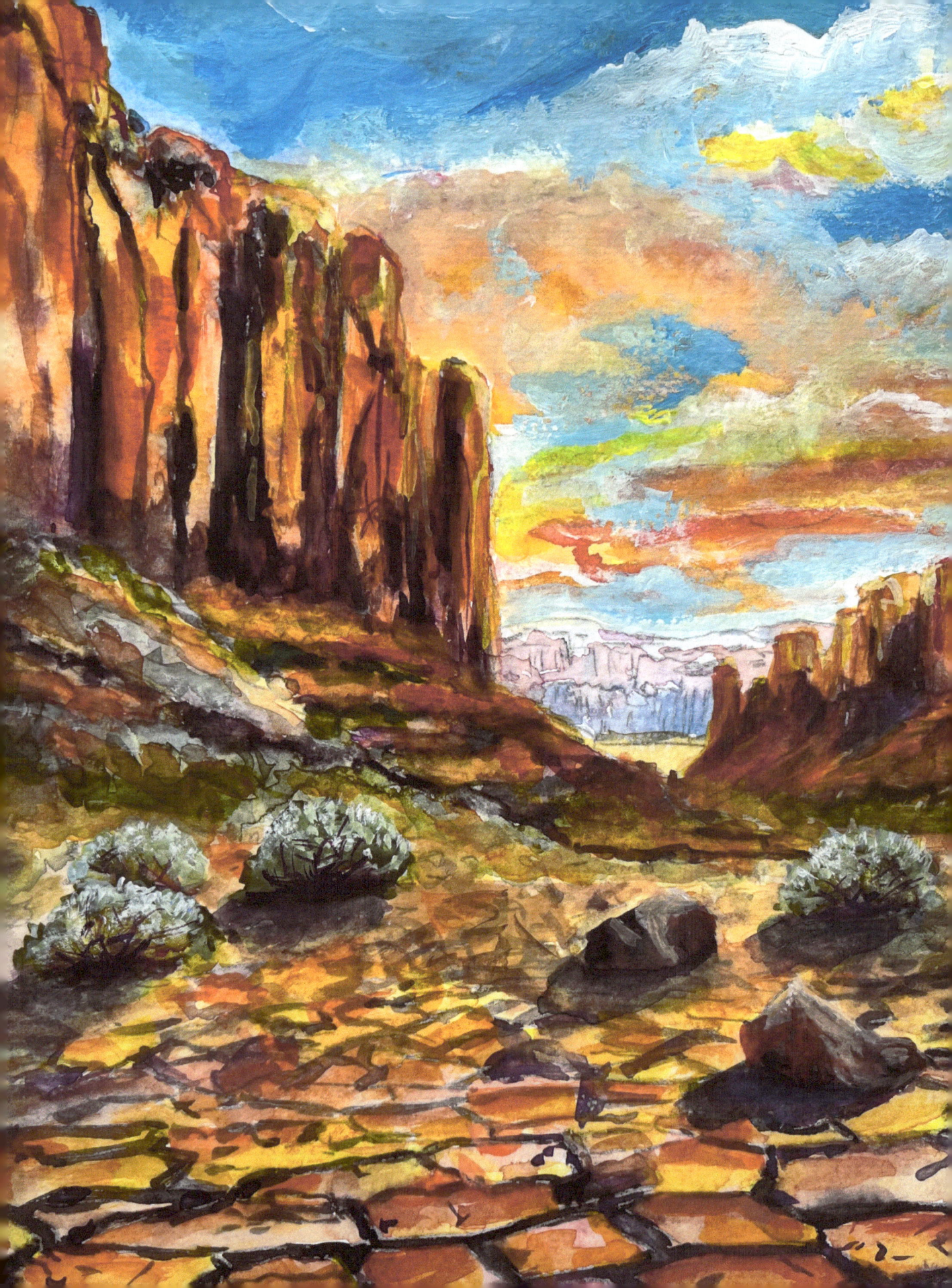

Psalm 63:1,5 (NLT)

O God, you are my God;
I earnestly search for you.
My soul thirsts for you; my whole body longs for you
in this parched and weary land where there is no water.

You satisfy me more than the richest feast.
I will praise you with songs of joy.

I lift my hands in prayer to you.
I am waiting for your help,
like a dry land waiting for rain. Selah
Psalm 143:6 (ERV)

Now on the last and most important day of the feast,
Jesus stood and called out [in a loud voice],
"If anyone is thirsty,
let him come to Me and drink!
John 7:37 (AMP)

They will hunger no longer, nor thirst anymore;
nor will the sun beat down on them, nor any [scorching] heat;

for the Lamb who is in the center of the throne
will be their Shepherd,
and He will guide them to springs of the waters of life;
and God will wipe every tear from their eyes
[giving them eternal comfort]."
Revelation 7:16, 17 (AMP)

I Need You!

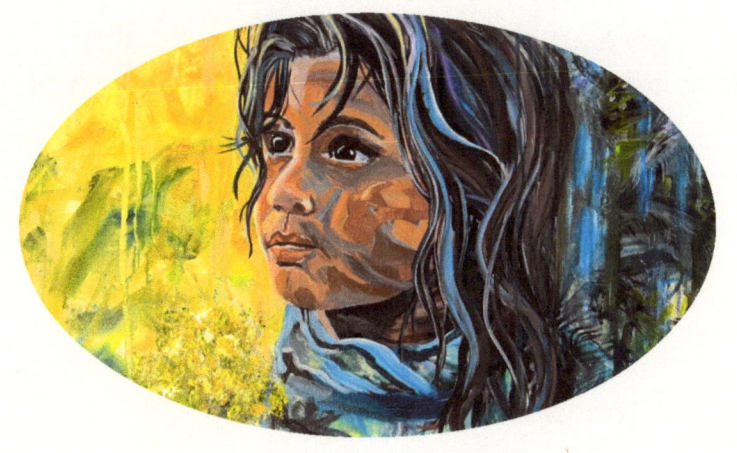

Psalm 42:1-3 (AMP)

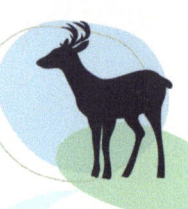

As the deer pants [longingly]
for the water brooks,
So my soul pants [longingly] for You, O God.

My soul (my life, my inner self) thirsts for God, for the living God.
When will I come and see the face of God?

My tears have been my food day and night,
While they say to me all day long, "Where is your God?"

I long and yearn for the courts of the Lord;
my heart and flesh cry out for the living God.
Psalm 84:2 (CSB)

The Spirit and the bride say, "Come."
Let anyone who hears this say, "Come."
Let anyone who is thirsty come.
Let anyone who desires drink freely from the water of life.
Revelation 22:17 (NLT)

"Blessed [forgiven, refreshed by God's grace] are those who mourn
[over their sins and repent], for they will be comforted[when the
burden of sin is lifted].
Matt. 5:4 (AMP)

God blesses you who are hungry now,
for you will be satisfied.
God blesses you who weep now,
for in due time you will laugh. Luke 6:21 (NLT)

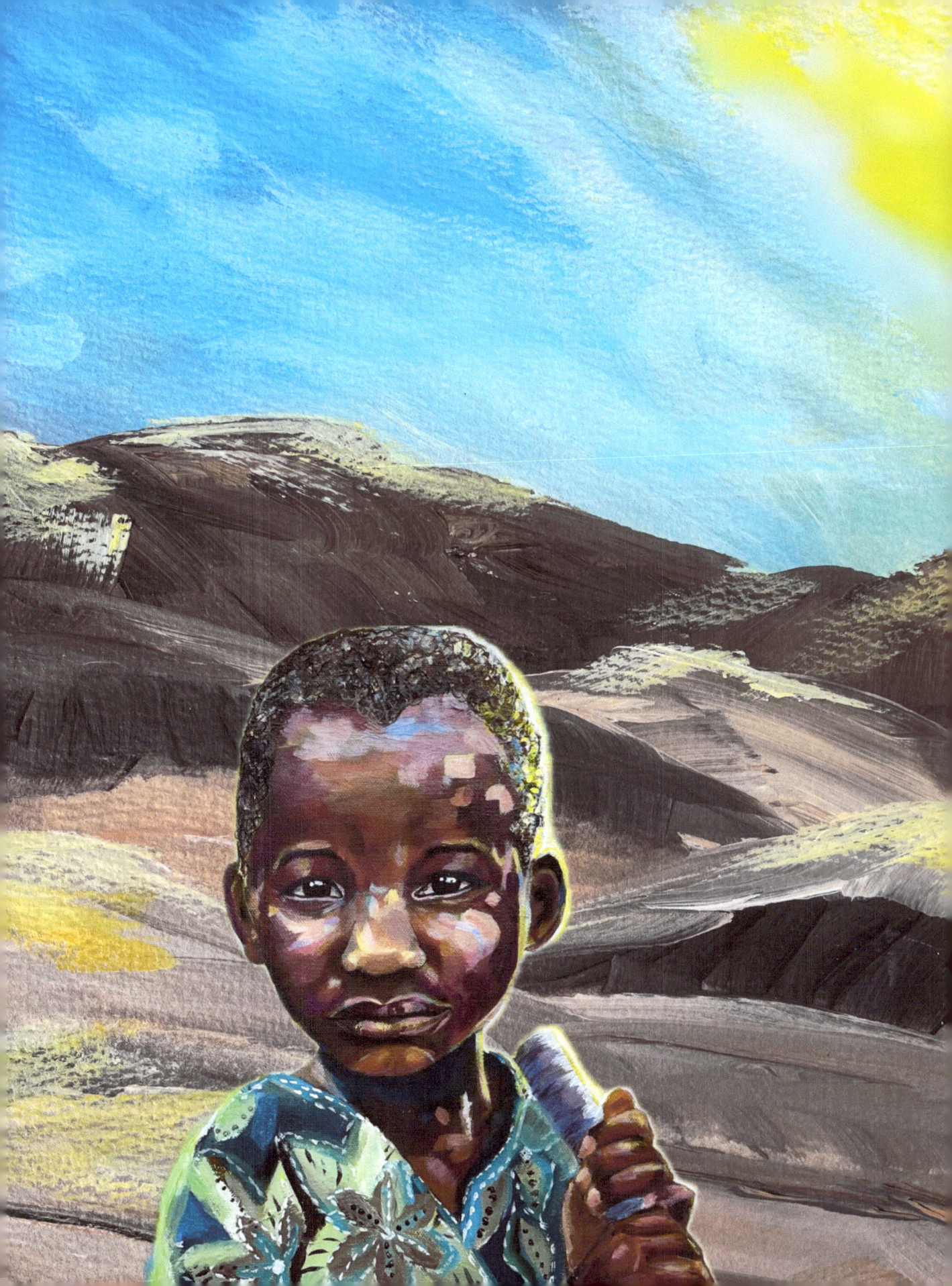

Psalm 42:6a-8,11 (NLV)

O my God, my soul is troubled within me.
So I remember You - -

Sea calls to sea at the sound of Your waterfalls.
All Your waves have rolled over me.

The Lord will send His loving-kindness in the day.
And His song will be with me in the night, a prayer to the God of my life.

Why are you sad, O my soul? Why have you become troubled within me?
Hope in God, for I will yet praise Him, my help and my God.

You are a hiding place for me.
You protect me from my troubles.
You surround me and protect me,
so I sing about the way you saved me. Selah
Psalm 32:7 (ERV)

'For I will restore health to you
And I will heal your wounds,' says the Lord,
'Because they have called you an outcast, saying:
"This is Zion; no one seeks her and no one cares for her."'
Jeremiah 30:17 (AMP)

May the God of hope fill you with all joy and peace in believing
[through the experience of your faith]
that by the power of the Holy Spirit
you will abound in hope and overflow
with confidence in His promises.
Romans 15:13 (AMP)

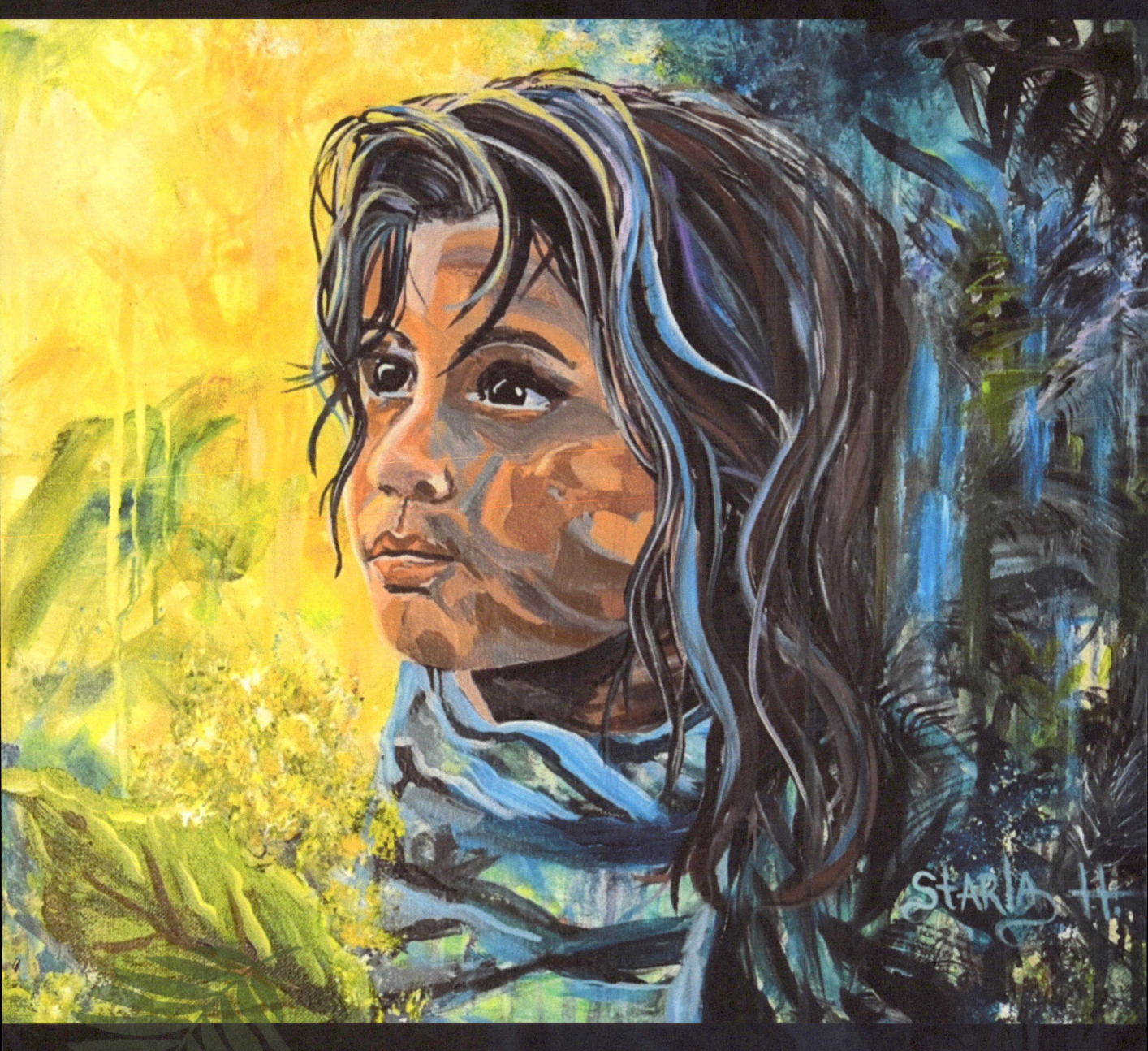

Why am I discouraged?
Why is my heart so sad?
I will put my hope in God!
I will praise him again— my Savior and my God!
Psalm 42:5 (NLT)

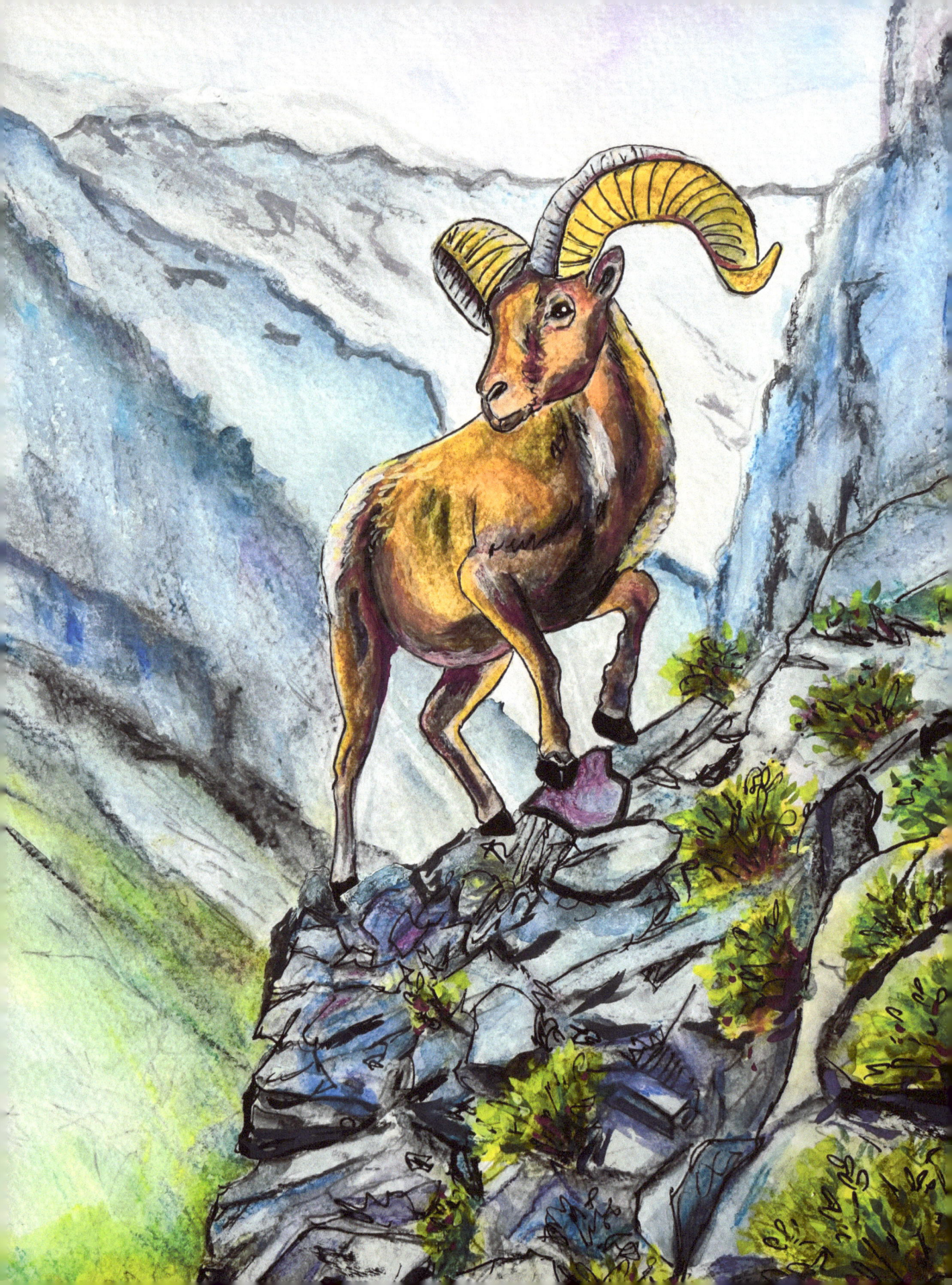

Psalm 94:16-18 (NLT)

**Who will protect me
from the wicked?
Who will stand up for me
against evildoers?
Unless the Lord had helped me,
I would soon have settled in the silence of the grave.
I cried out, "I am slipping!"
but your unfailing love, O Lord, supported me.**

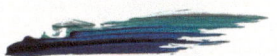

But as for me, my feet came close to stumbling,
My steps had almost slipped.
Psalm 73:2 (AMP)

A person's steps are established by the Lord,
and he takes pleasure in his way.
Though he falls, he will not be overwhelmed,
because the Lord supports him with his hand.
Psalm 37:23, 24 (CSB)

Uphold me according to Your word [of promise], so that I may live;
And do not let me be ashamed
of my hope [in Your great goodness].
Uphold me that I may be safe,
That I may have regard for Your statutes continually.
Psalm 119:116, 117 (AMP)

But I prayed for you, Shim'on,
that your trust might not fail.
And you, once you have turned back in repentance,
strengthen your brothers!" Luke 22:32 (CJB)

Psalm 17:6-8 (NLT)

I am praying to you
because I know you will answer, O God.
Bend down and listen as I pray.

Show me your unfailing love in wonderful ways.
By your mighty power you rescue
those who seek refuge from their enemies.

Guard me as you would guard your own eyes.
Hide me in the shadow of your wings.

God, hear my prayer;
listen to the words from my mouth.
Psalm 54:2 (CSB)

But rejoice, all who take refuge in You,
Sing for joy forever!
And may You shelter them,
That those who love Your name may rejoice in You.
For You bless the righteous person, Lord,
You surround him with favor as with a shield.
Psalm 5:11,12 (NASB)

You can go to him for protection.
He will cover you like a bird spreading its wings over its babies.
You can trust him to surround and protect you like a shield.
Psalm 91:4 (ERV)

Nothing is more precious than your loving kindness.
All people can find protection close to you.
Psalm 36:7 (ERV)

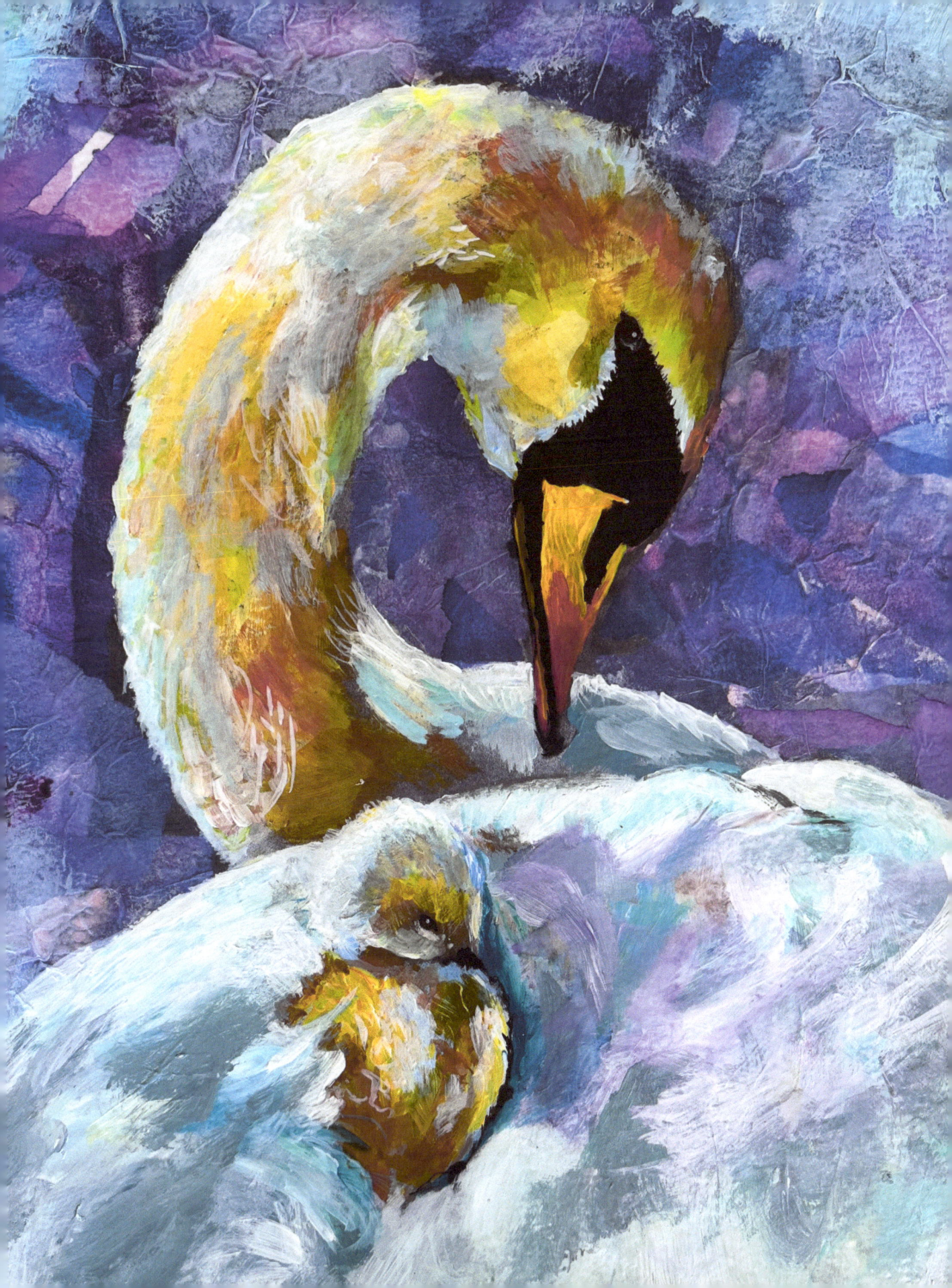

Psalm 63:6-8 (NLV)

On my bed I remember You.
I think of You through the hours of the night.

For You have been my help.
And I sing for joy in the shadow of Your wings.

My soul holds on to You.
Your right hand holds me up.

My eyes wait for the night hours,
so I may think about Your Word.
Psalm 119:48 (NLV)

But his delight is in the law of the Lord,
And on His law [His precepts and teachings]
he [habitually] meditates day and night.
Psalm 1:2 (AMP)

But let all who take refuge in you rejoice;
let them sing joyful praises forever.
Spread your protection over them,
that all who love your name may be filled with joy.
Psalm 5:11, 12 (NLT)

"Let his left hand be under my head
And his right hand embrace me."
Song of Solomon 2:6 (AMP)

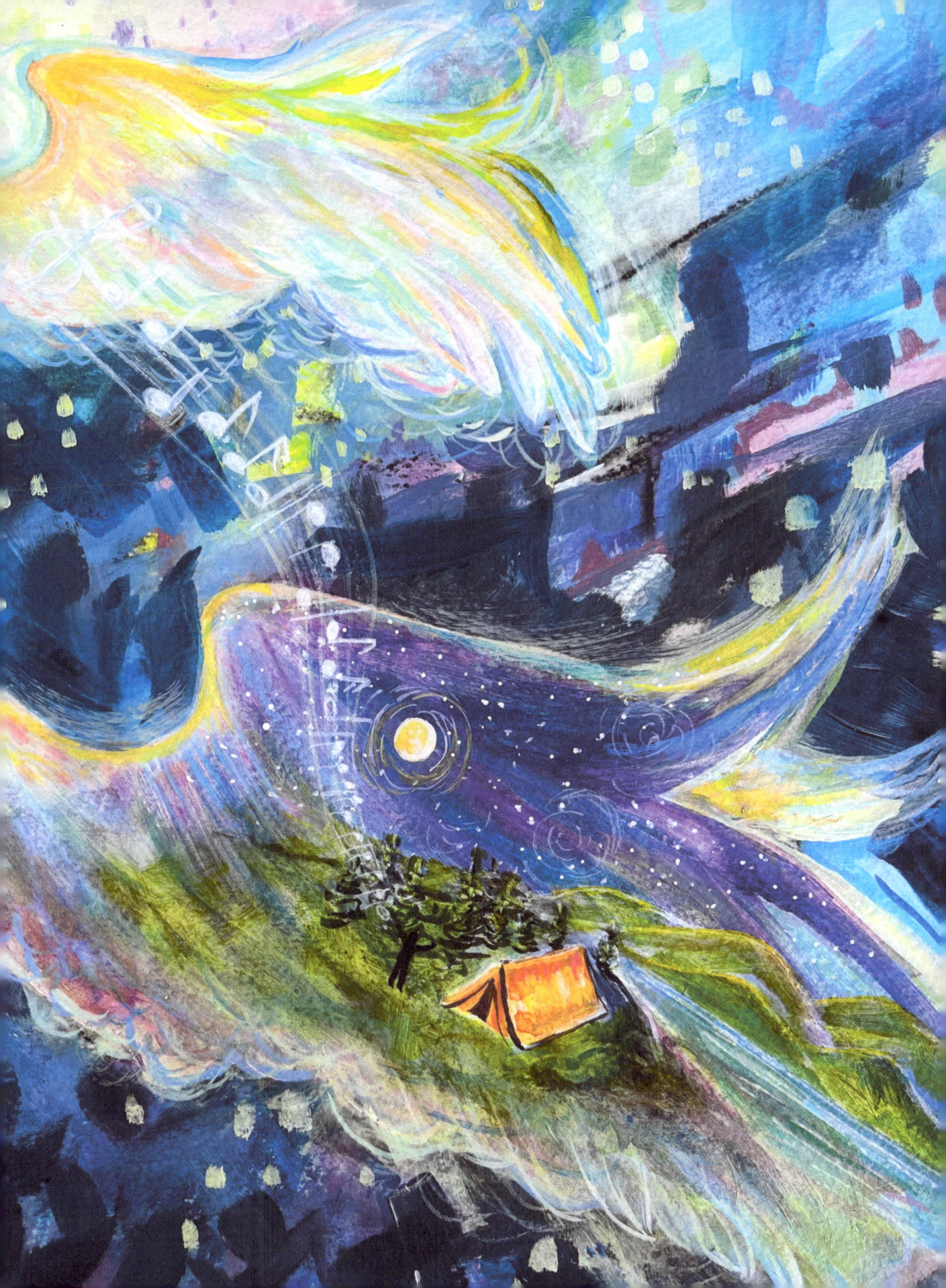

Be Still, My Heart

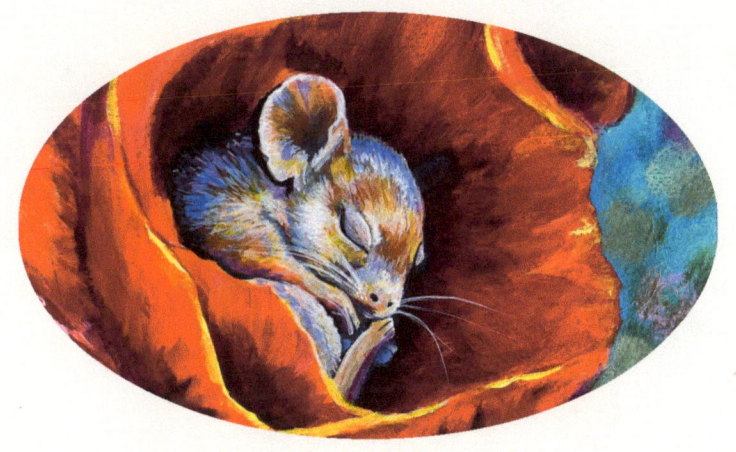

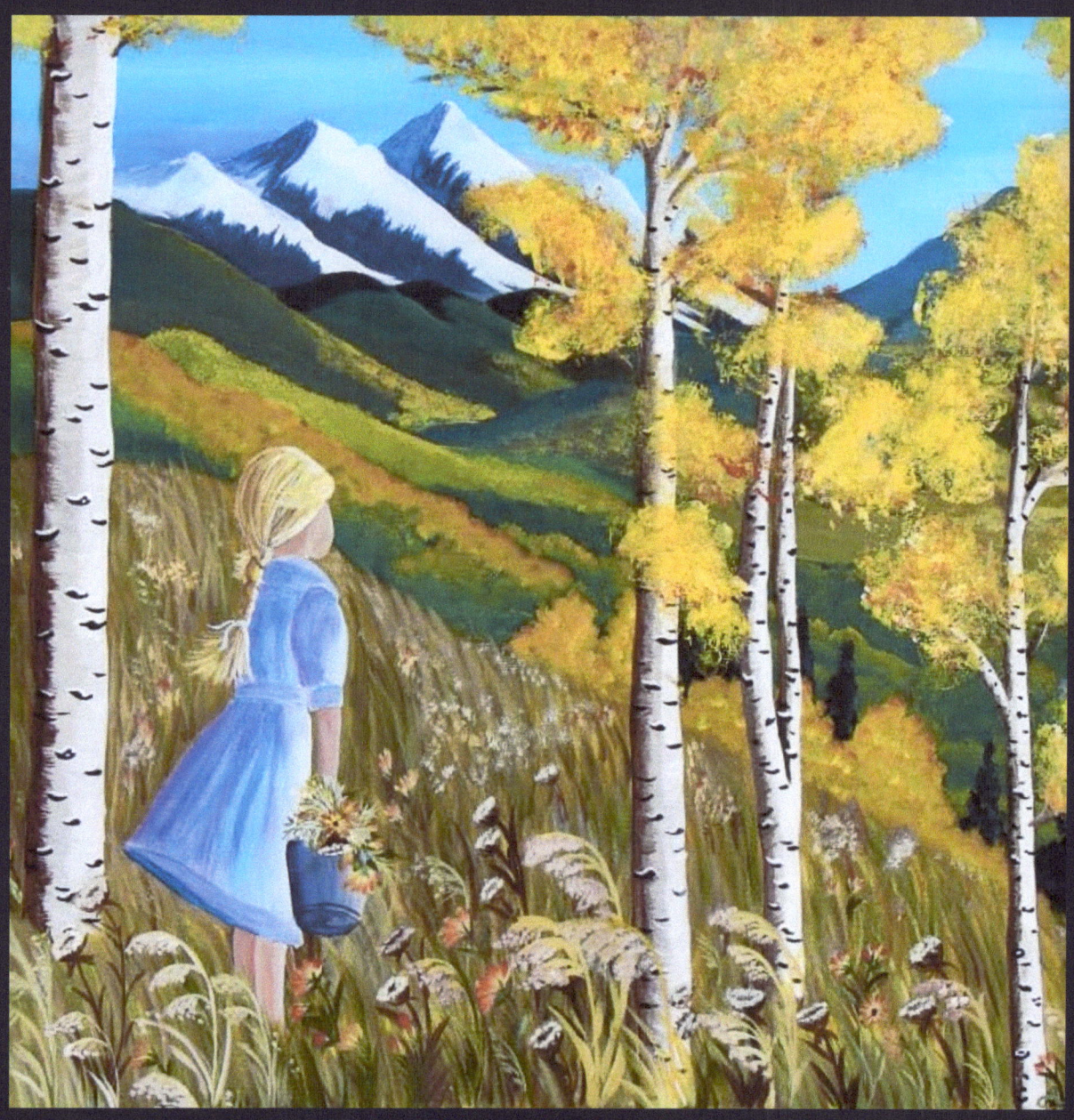

"Be still and know (recognize, understand) that I am God.
I will be exalted among the nations!
I will be exalted in the earth."   Psalm 46:10 (AMP)

Know that the Lord is God.
He made us, and we belong to him.
We are his people, the sheep he takes care of Psalm 100:3 (ERV).

The Lord will fight for you
while you [only need to] keep silent and remain calm."
Exodus 14:14 (AMP)

Proud people will stop being proud.
They will bow down to the ground with shame,
and only the Lord will still stand high.
Isaiah 2:11 (ERV)

"Listen to this, Job;
Stand still and consider the wonders of God.
Job 37:14 (AMP)

It is good that one should be quiet
and wait for the saving power of the Lord.
Lamentations 3:26 (NLV)

Let all the world look to me for salvation!
For I am God; there is no other.
Isaiah 45:22 (NLT)

Then they will know that your name is Yahweh—
that you alone are the Lord.
They will know that you are God Most High,
ruler over all the earth! Psalm 83:18 (ERV)

Psalm 62:5-8 NLV

My soul is quiet
and waits for God alone.
My hope comes from Him.

He alone is my rock and the One Who saves me.
He is my strong place. I will not be shaken.

My being safe and my honor rest with God.
My safe place is in God, the rock of my strength.

Trust in Him at all times, O people.
Pour out your heart before Him.
God is a safe place for us.

But I will look to the Lord;
I will wait for the God of my salvation.
My God will hear me. Micah 7:7 (CSB)

There is no God except the Lord.
There is no Rock except our God.
God is the one who gives me strength.
He clears the path I need to take. Psalm 18:31,32 (ERV)

But you, Adonai, are a shield for me;
you are my glory, you lift my head high. Psalm 3:3 (CJB)

Do not worry. Learn to pray about everything.
Give thanks to God
as you ask Him for what you need.
Phil. 4:6 (NLV)

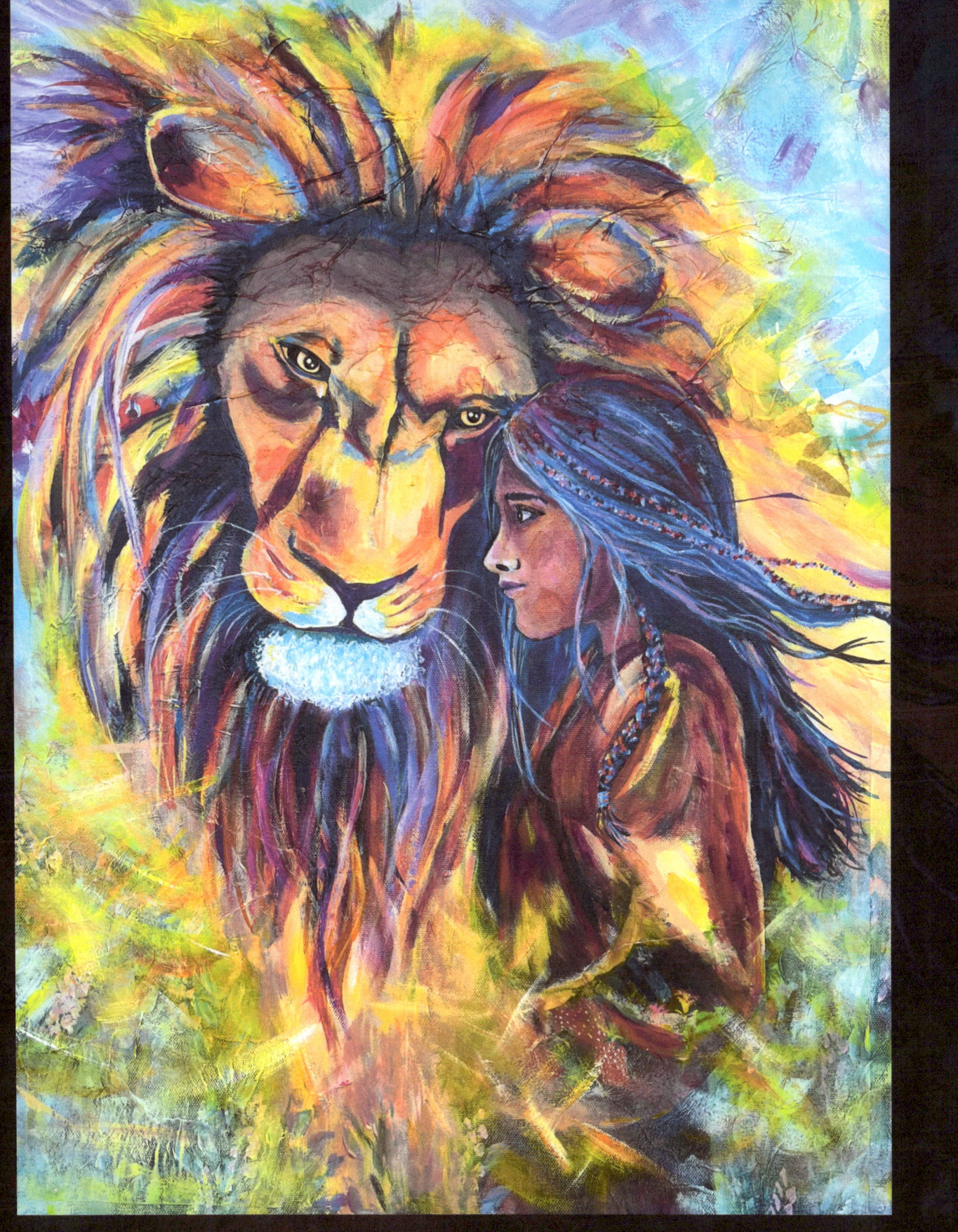

Psalm 4:8 (AMP)

**In peace [and with a tranquil heart]
I will both lie down and sleep,
For You alone, O Lord,
make me dwell in safety and confident trust.**

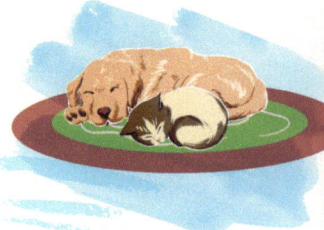

You can go to bed without fear;
you will lie down and sleep soundly. Proverbs 3:24 (NLT)

God, you give true peace to people who depend on you,
to those who trust in you. Isaiah 26:3 (ERV)

Peace I leave with you;
My [perfect] peace I give to you;
not as the world gives do I give to you.
Do not let your heart be troubled, nor let it be afraid.
[Let My perfect peace calm you in every circumstance
and give you courage and strength for every challenge.]
John 14:27 (AMP)

Those who live in the shelter of the Most High
will find rest in the shadow of the Almighty.
This I declare about the Lord:
He alone is my refuge, my place of safety;
he is my God, and I trust him. Psalm 91:1,2 (NLT)

Adonai is my shepherd; I lack nothing.
He has me lie down in grassy pastures,
he leads me by quiet water,
he restores my inner person.
He guides me in right paths
for the sake of his own name. Psalm 23:1-3 (CJB)

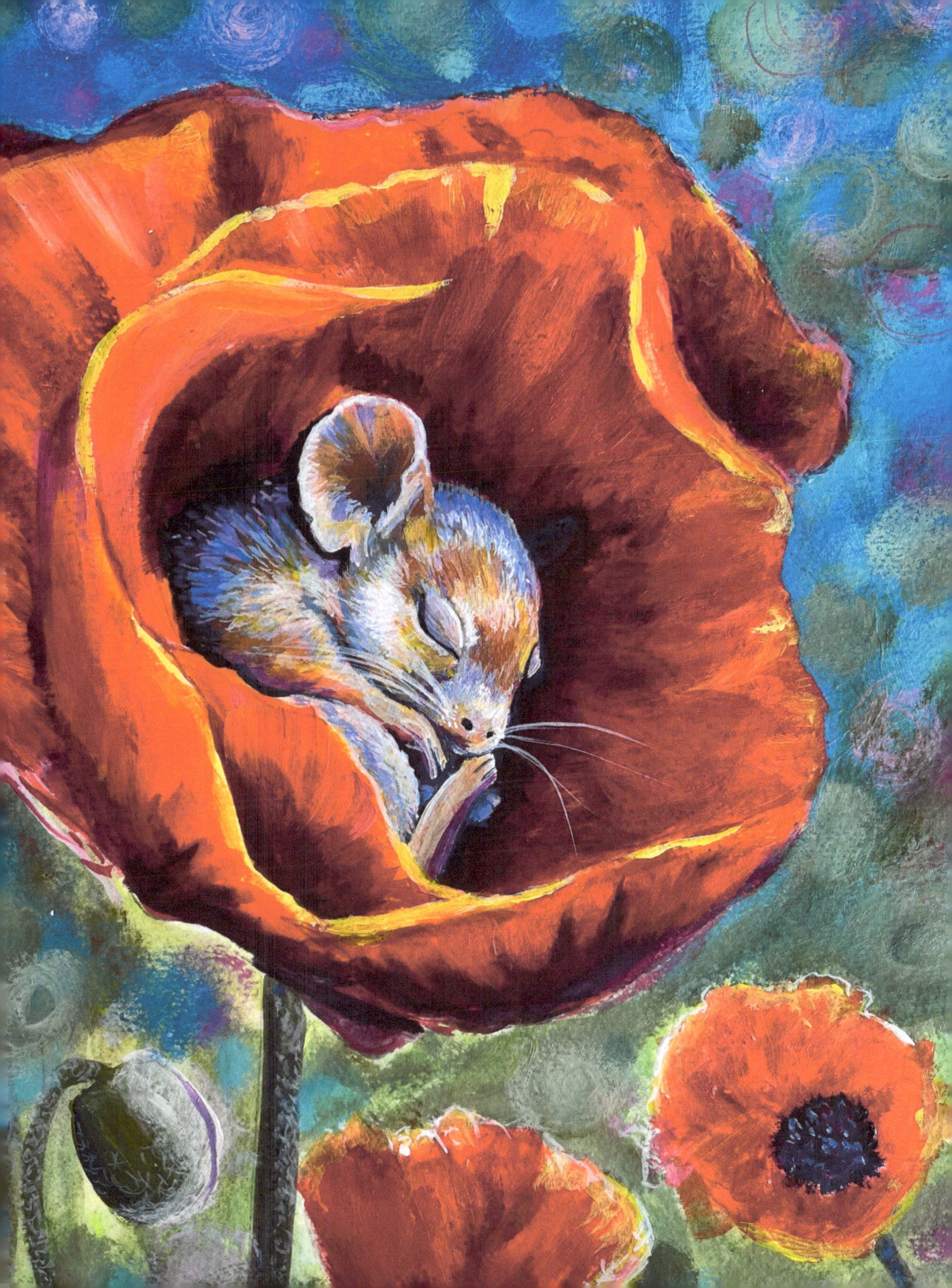

Psalm 94:19 (NLV)

**When my worry is great within me,
Your comfort brings joy to my soul.**

He comforts us every time we have trouble
so that when others have trouble,
we can comfort them with the same comfort God gives us.
We share in the many sufferings of Christ.
In the same way, much comfort comes to us through Christ.
2 Cor. 1:4,5 (ERV)

I have seen their ways, and I will heal them;
I will lead them and give comfort
to them and to those who mourn for them
I will create the right words:
'Shalom shalom to those far off
and to those nearby!' says Adonai;
'I will heal them!'" Isaiah 57:18, 19 (CJB)

I will comfort you as one is comforted by his mother.
And you will be comforted in Jerusalem."
Isaiah 66:13 (NLV)

This is my comfort in my affliction,
That Your word has revived me and given me life.
Psalm 119:50 (AMP)

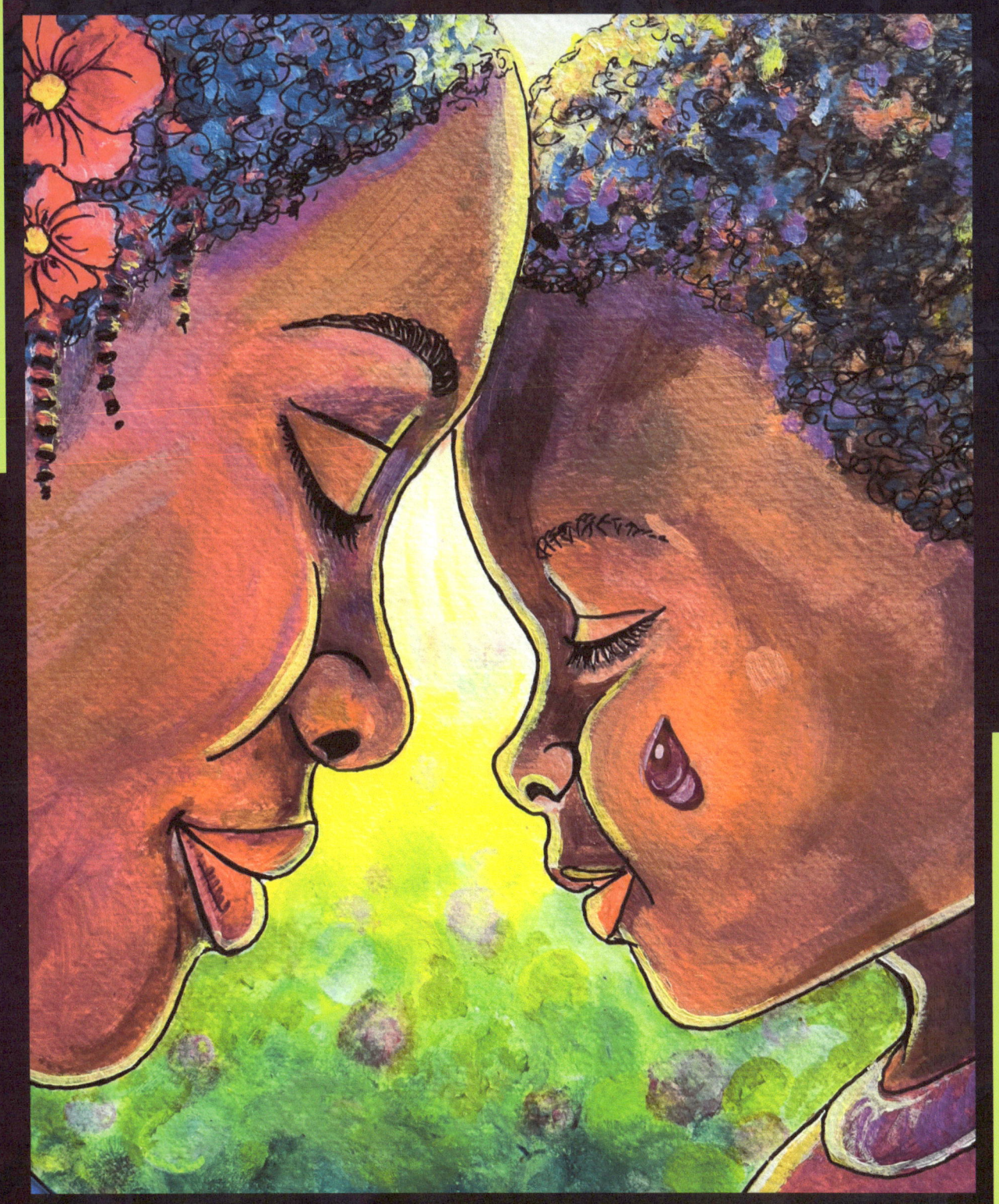

**You keep track of all my sorrows,
(my wanderings)
You have collected all my tears in your bottle.
You have recorded each one in your book.**

Psalm 56:8 (NLT)

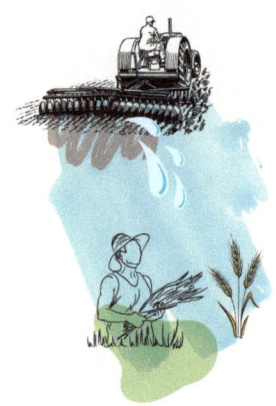

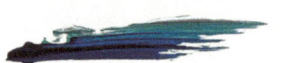

Those who plant in tears
will harvest with shouts of joy.
They weep as they go to plant their seed,
but they sing as they return with the harvest.
Psalm 126:5,6 (NLT)

Then those who feared the Lord spoke to one another,
and the Lord listened attentively and heard it,
and a book of remembrance was written before Him for
those who fear the Lord and esteem His name.
Mal. 3:16 (NASB)

"Return to Hezekiah the leader of My people.
Tell him, 'This is what the Lord, the God of your father David, says,
"I have heard your prayer. I have seen your tears.
See, I will heal you.
On the third day you must go up to the house of the Lord.
2 Kings 20:5 (NLV)

The Lamb in front of the throne will be their shepherd.
He will lead them to springs of water that give life.
And God will wipe away every tear from their eyes."
Revelation 7:17 (ERV)

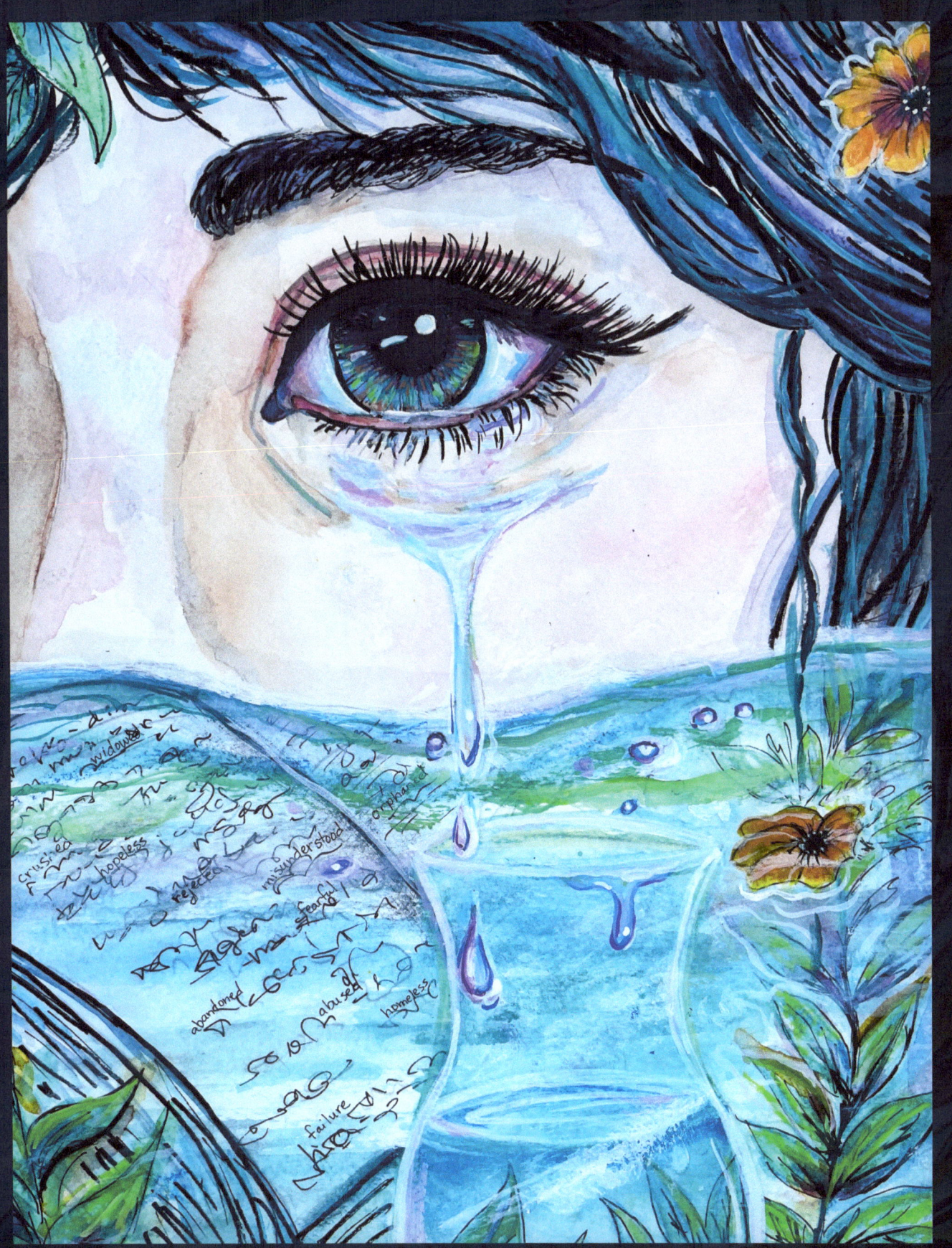

The Savior Is Near

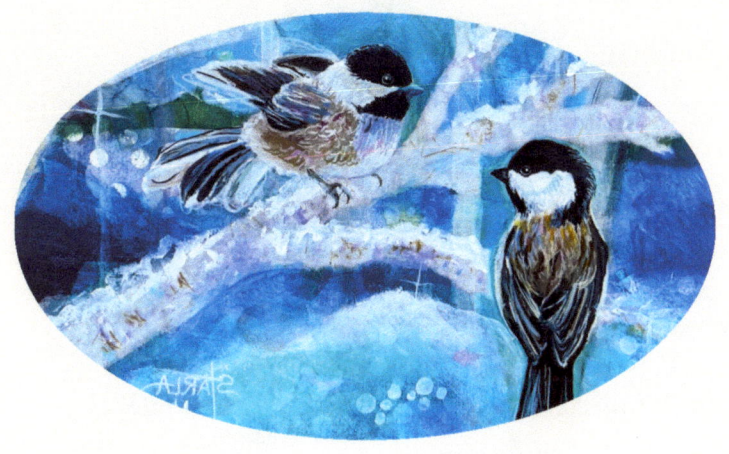

Psalm 71:20 (CSB)

You caused me to experience
many troubles and misfortunes,
but you will revive me again.
You will bring me up again,
even from the depths of the earth.

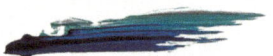

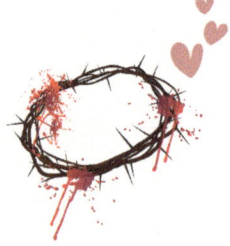

For Your loving-kindness toward me is great.
And You have saved my soul
from the bottom of the grave. Psalm 86:13 (NLV)

Though I walk in the midst of trouble, You will revive me;
You will stretch out Your hand against the wrath of my enemies,
And Your right hand will save me. Psalm 138:7 (AMP)

Even when I walk
through the darkest valley, (the dark valley of death)
I will not be afraid,
for you are close beside me.
Your rod and your staff
protect and comfort me. Psalm 23:4 (NLT)

One who is righteous has many adversities,
but the Lord rescues him from them all.
Psalm 34:19 (CSB)

Turn my eyes from worthless things,
and give me life through your word. (in your ways)
Psalm 119:37 (NLT)

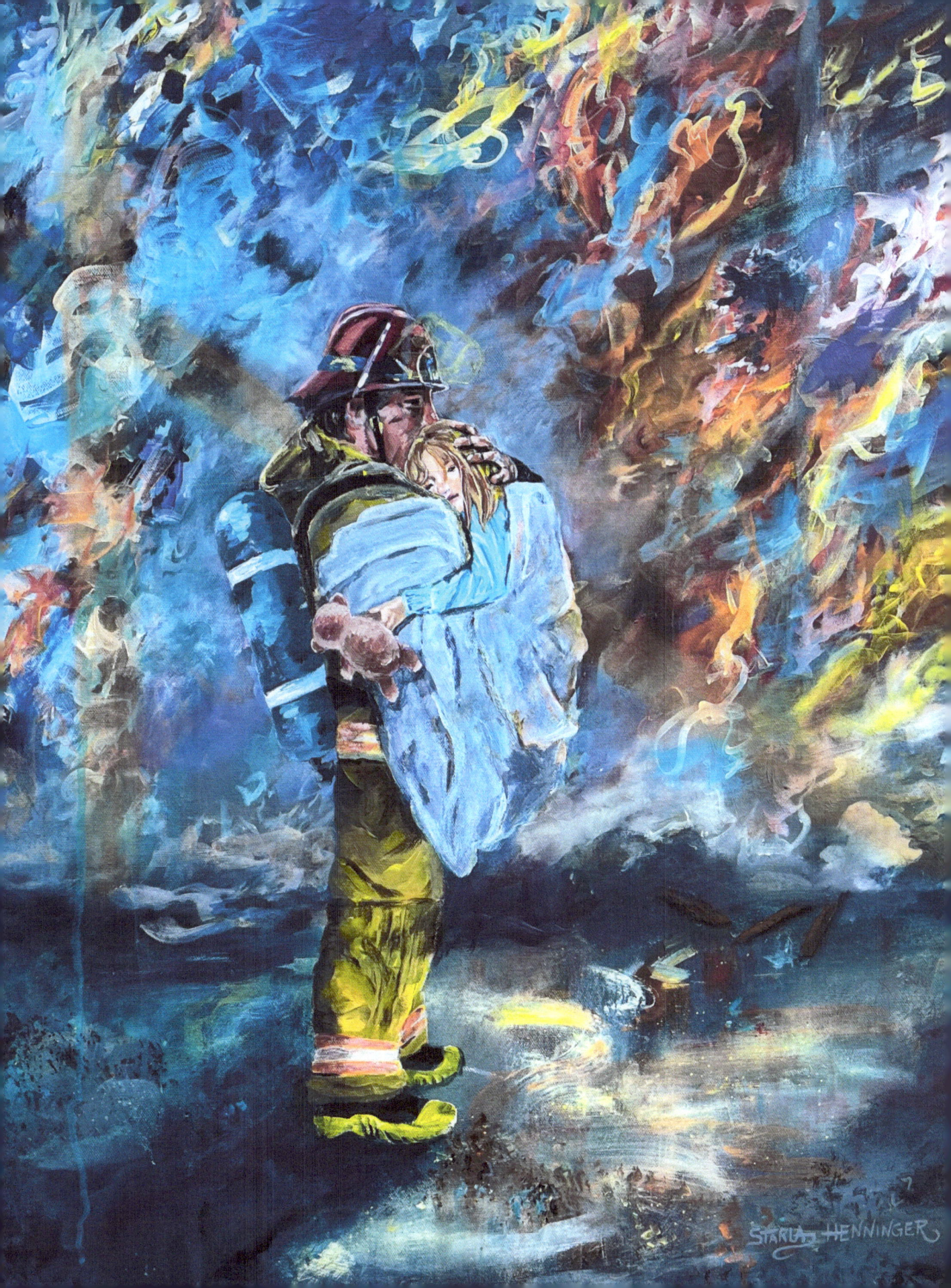

Psalm 147:3 (AMP)

**He heals the brokenhearted
And binds up their wounds
[healing their pain
and comforting their sorrow].**

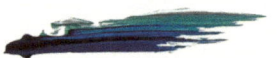

The Lord is near the brokenhearted;
he saves those crushed in spirit. Psalm 34:18 (CSB)

"Come to Me, all who are weary and heavily burdened
[by religious rituals that provide no peace],
and I will give you rest [refreshing your souls with salvation].
Take My yoke upon you
and learn from Me
[following Me as My disciple],
for I am gentle and humble in heart,
and you will find rest (renewal, blessed quiet)
for your souls. Matt. 11:28, 29 (AMP)

For the High and Exalted One,
who lives forever, whose name is holy, says this:
"I live in a high and holy place,
and with the oppressed and lowly of spirit,
to revive the spirit of the lowly
and revive the heart of the oppressed.
Isaiah 57:15 (CSB)

The gifts on an altar that God wants are a broken spirit. O God,
You will not hate a broken heart
and a heart with no pride. Psalm 51:17 (NLV)

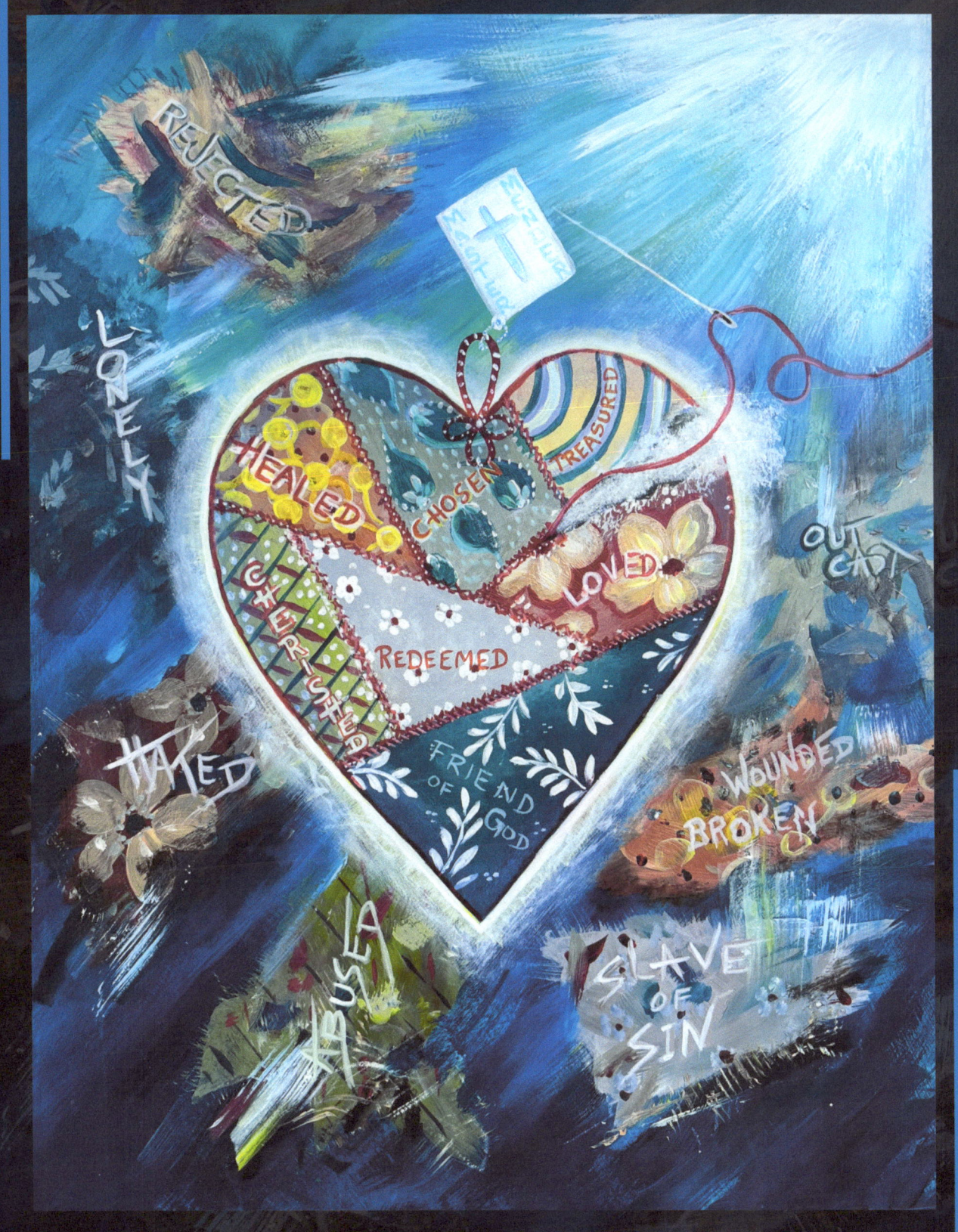

Psalm 66:9, 10, 12 (CSB)

He keeps us alive
and does not allow our feet to slip.

For you, God, tested us;
you refined us as silver is refined.

You let men ride over our heads;
we went through fire and water,
but you brought us out to abundance.

When you go through deep waters, I will be with you.
When you go through rivers of difficulty, you will not drown.
When you walk through the fire of oppression,
you will not be burned up; the flames will not consume you.
Isaiah 43:2 (NLT)

Do not fear [anything], for I am with you;
Do not be afraid, for I am your God.
I will strengthen you, be assured I will help you;
I will certainly take hold of you with My righteous right hand
[a hand of justice, of power, of victory, of salvation].'   Isaiah 41:10 (AMP)

With this hope you can be happy even if you need to have sorrow
and all kinds of tests for awhile.
These tests have come to prove your faith and to show that it is good. Gold,
which can be destroyed, is tested by fire.
Your faith is worth much more than gold and it must be tested also.
Then your faith will bring thanks and shining-greatness and honor
to Jesus Christ when He comes again.
I Peter 1:6, 7 (NLV)

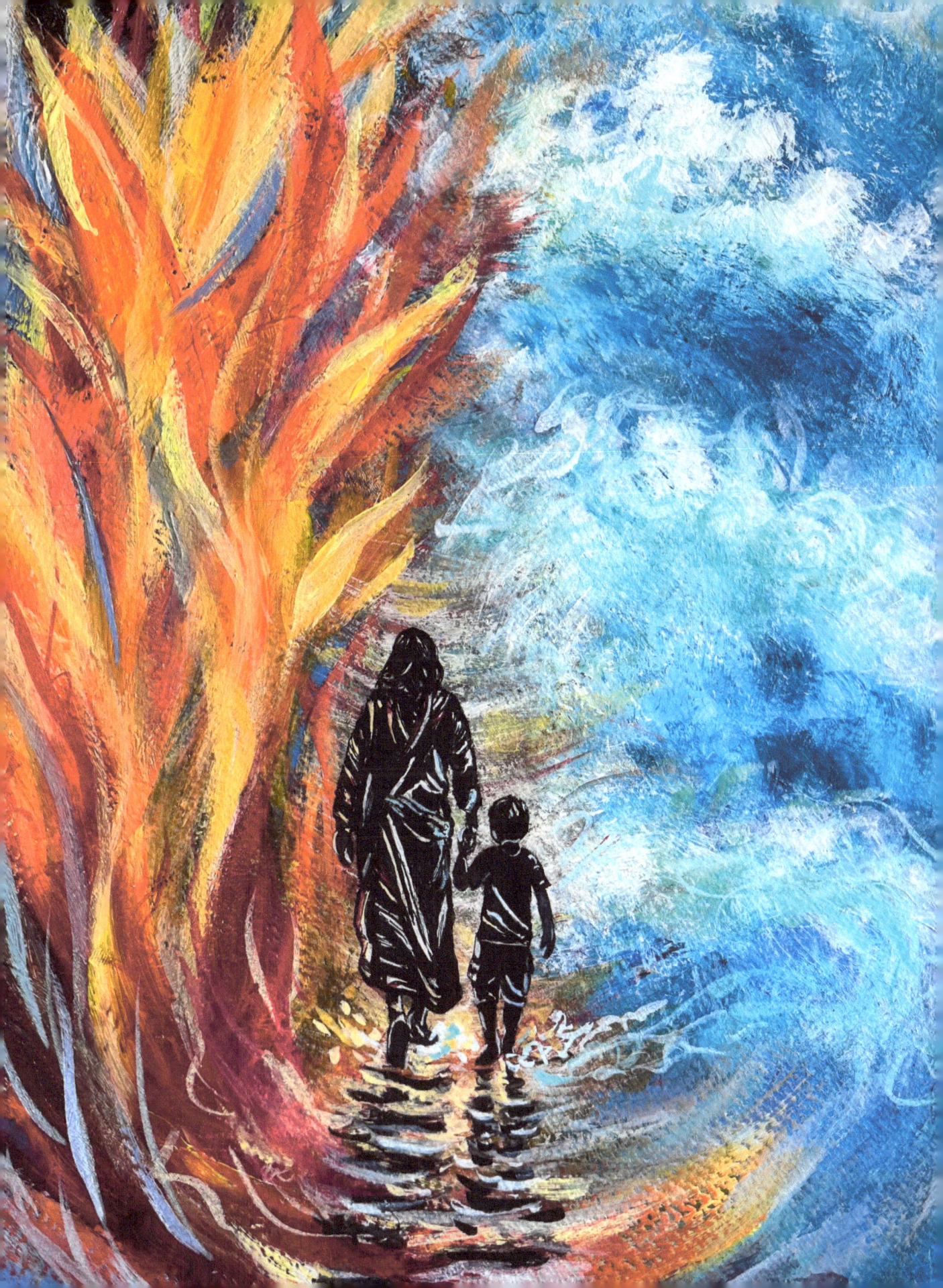

Psalm 55:22 (CSB)

**Cast your burden on the Lord,
and he will sustain you;
he will never allow the righteous to be shaken.**

Casting all your cares [all your anxieties,
all your worries, and all your concerns,
once and for all] on Him,
for He cares about you [with deepest affection,
and watches over you very carefully]. I Peter 5:7 (AMP)

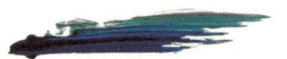

Consider the birds of the sky:
They don't sow or reap or gather into barns,
yet your heavenly Father feeds them.
Aren't you worth more than they?
Can any of you add one moment to his life span by worrying?
But seek first the kingdom of God and his righteousness,
and all these things will be provided for you.
Matt. 6:26, 27, 33 (CSB)

Peace I leave with you; My [perfect] peace I give to you;
not as the world gives do I give to you.
Do not let your heart be troubled, nor let it be afraid.
[Let My perfect peace calm you in every circumstance
and give you courage and strength for every challenge.]
John 14:27 (AMP)

Praise the Lord!
Every day he helps us with the loads we must carry.
He is the God who saves us. Selah. Psalm 68:19 (ERV)

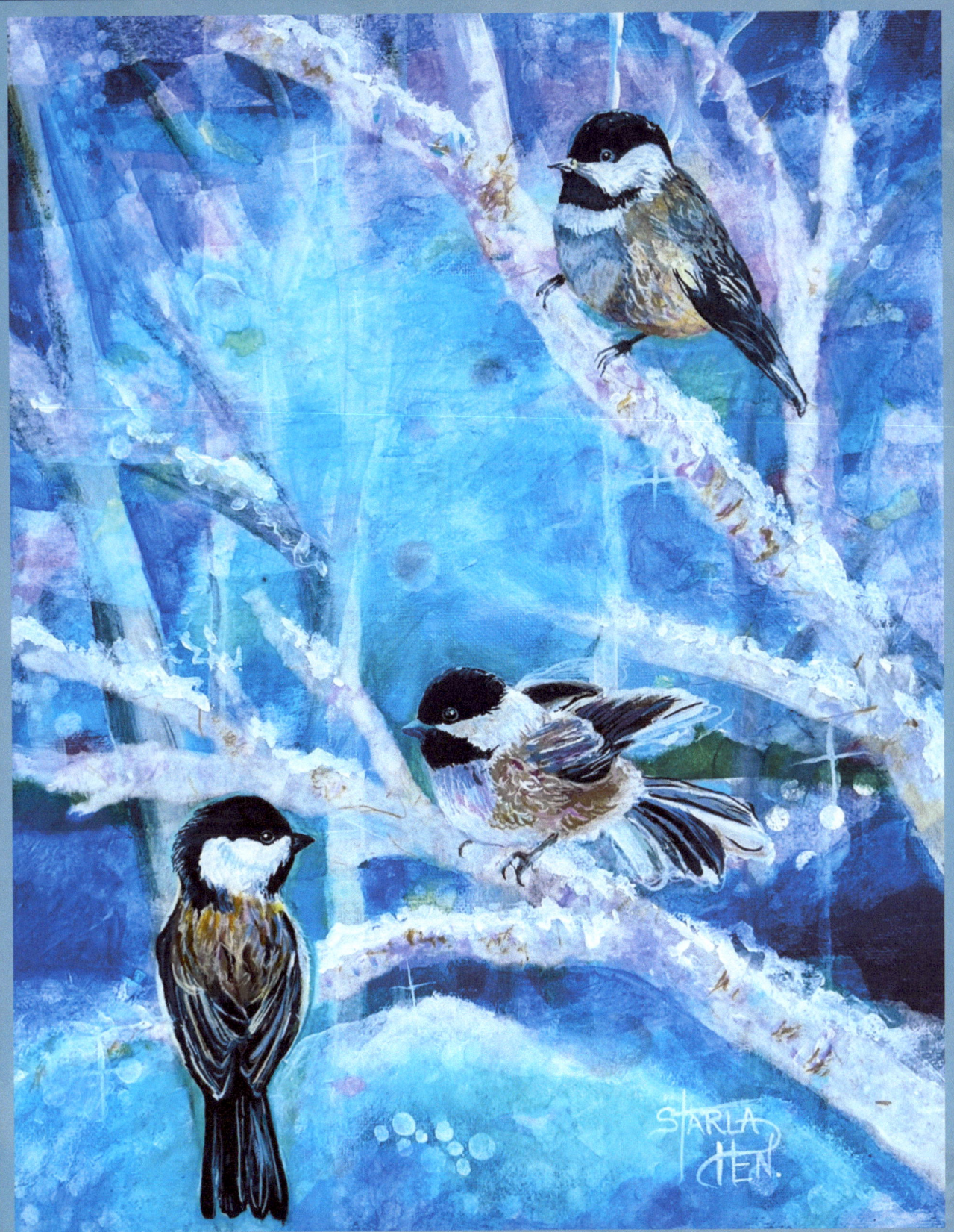

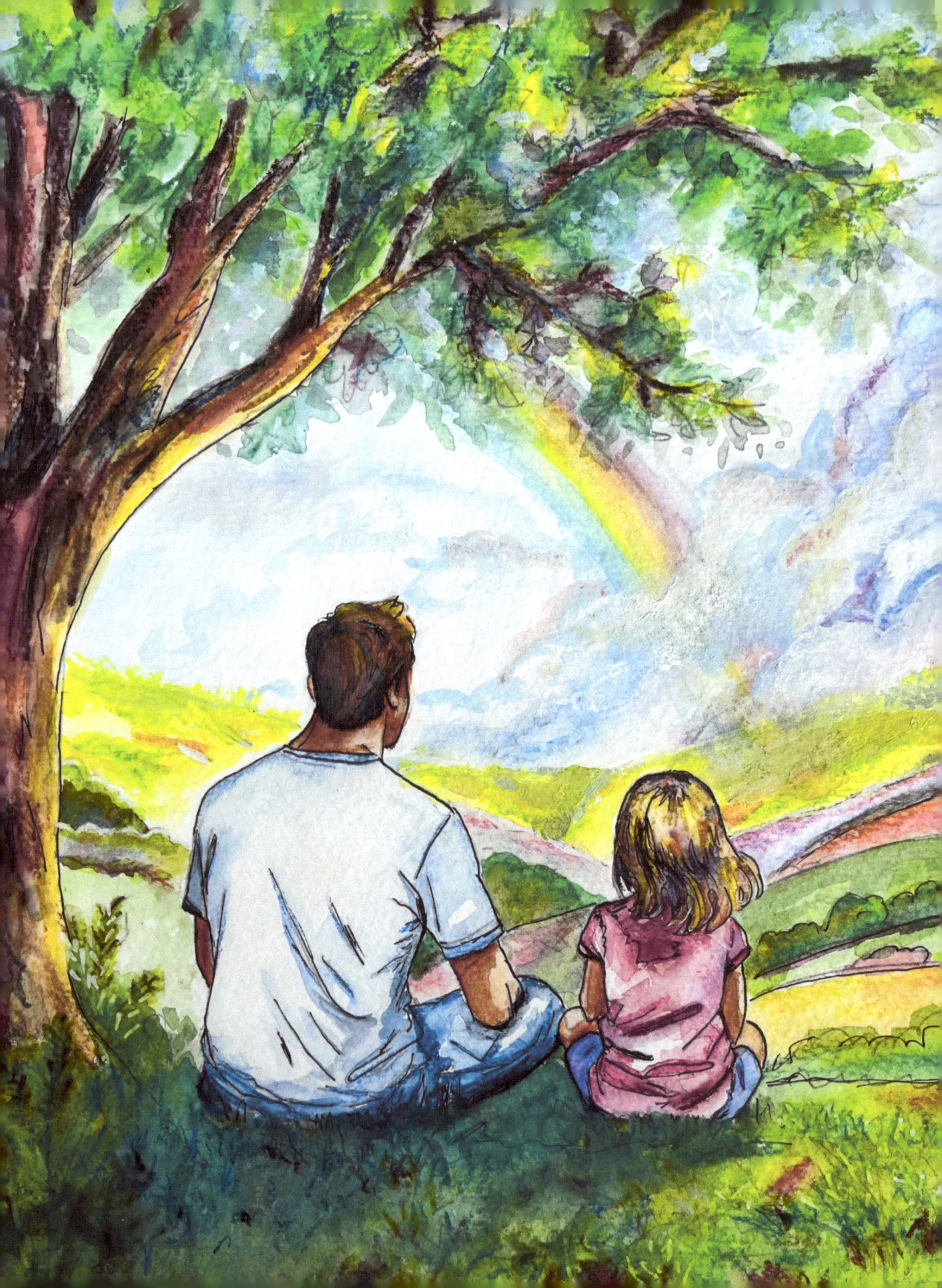

Psalm 73:28 (AMP)

But as for me,
it is good for me to draw near to God;
I have made the Lord God my refuge and placed my trust in Him,
that I may tell of all Your works.

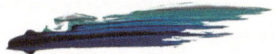

So you should look for the Lord before it is too late.
You should call to him now, while he is near. Isaiah 55:6 (ERV)

Come close to God, and God will come close to you.
Wash your hands, you sinners; purify your hearts,
for your loyalty is divided between God and the world.
James 4:8 (NLT)

Sprinkled with the blood of Christ,
our hearts have been made free from a guilty conscience,
and our bodies have been washed with pure water.
So come near to God with a sincere heart,
full of confidence because of our faith in Christ. Hebrews 10:22 (ERV)

But more than that, I count everything as loss
compared to the priceless privilege and supreme advantage
of knowing Christ Jesus my Lord
[and of growing more deeply
and thoroughly acquainted with Him-—a joy unequaled].
For His sake I have lost everything,
and I consider it all garbage,
so that I may gain Christ, Phil. 3:8 (AMP)

O taste and see that the Lord is good.
How happy is the man who trusts in Him! Psalm 34:8 (NLV)

His Plans Are Good

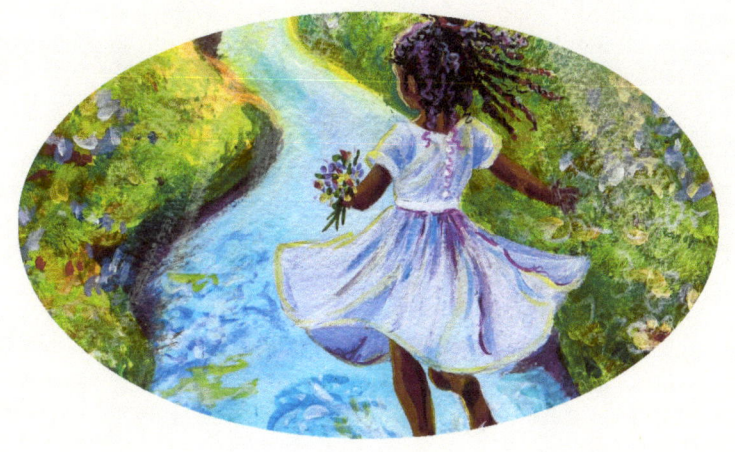

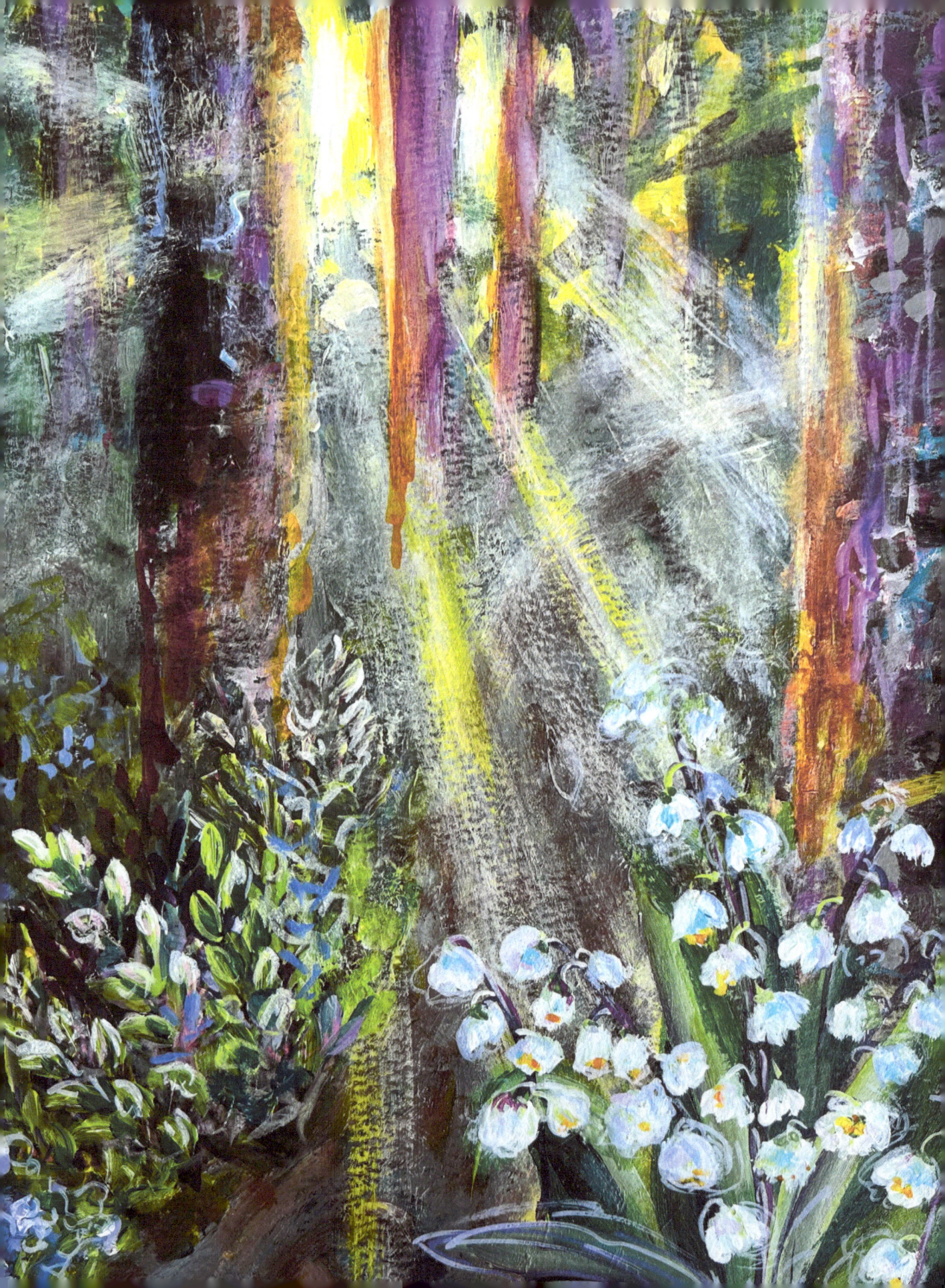

Psalm 143:8 (ERV)

**Show me your faithful love this morning.
I trust in you.
Show me what I should do.
I put my life in your hands!   Psalm 143:8 (ERV)**

> Show me the right path, O Lord;
> point out the road for me to follow.
> Lead me by your truth and teach me,
> for you are the God who saves me.
> All day long I put my hope in you.
> Psalm 25:4,5 (NLT)
>
> I will lead the blind by a way they did not know;
> I will guide them on paths they have not known.
> I will turn darkness to light in front of them
> and rough places into level ground.
> This is what I will do for them,
> and I will not abandon them.
> Isaiah 42:16 (CSB)
>
> Lord, I know that our lives do not belong to us.
> We have no control over what happens.
> Jeremiah 10:23 (ERV)
>
> Jesus told him, "I am the way, the truth, and the life.
> No one can come to the Father except through me.
> John 14:26 (NLT)

Psalm 121:1-8 (NLV)

I will lift up my eyes
to the mountains.
Where will my help come from?

My help comes from the Lord,
Who made heaven and earth.

He will not let your feet go out from under you.
He Who watches over you will not sleep.

Listen, He Who watches over Israel
will not close his eyes or sleep.

The Lord watches over you.
The Lord is your safe cover at your right hand.

The sun will not hurt you during the day
and the moon will not hurt you during the night.

The Lord will keep you from all that is sinful.
He will watch over your soul.

The Lord will watch over your coming and going,
now and forever.

Trust in the Lord with all your heart;
do not depend on your own understanding.

Seek his will in all you do,
and he will show you which path to take.

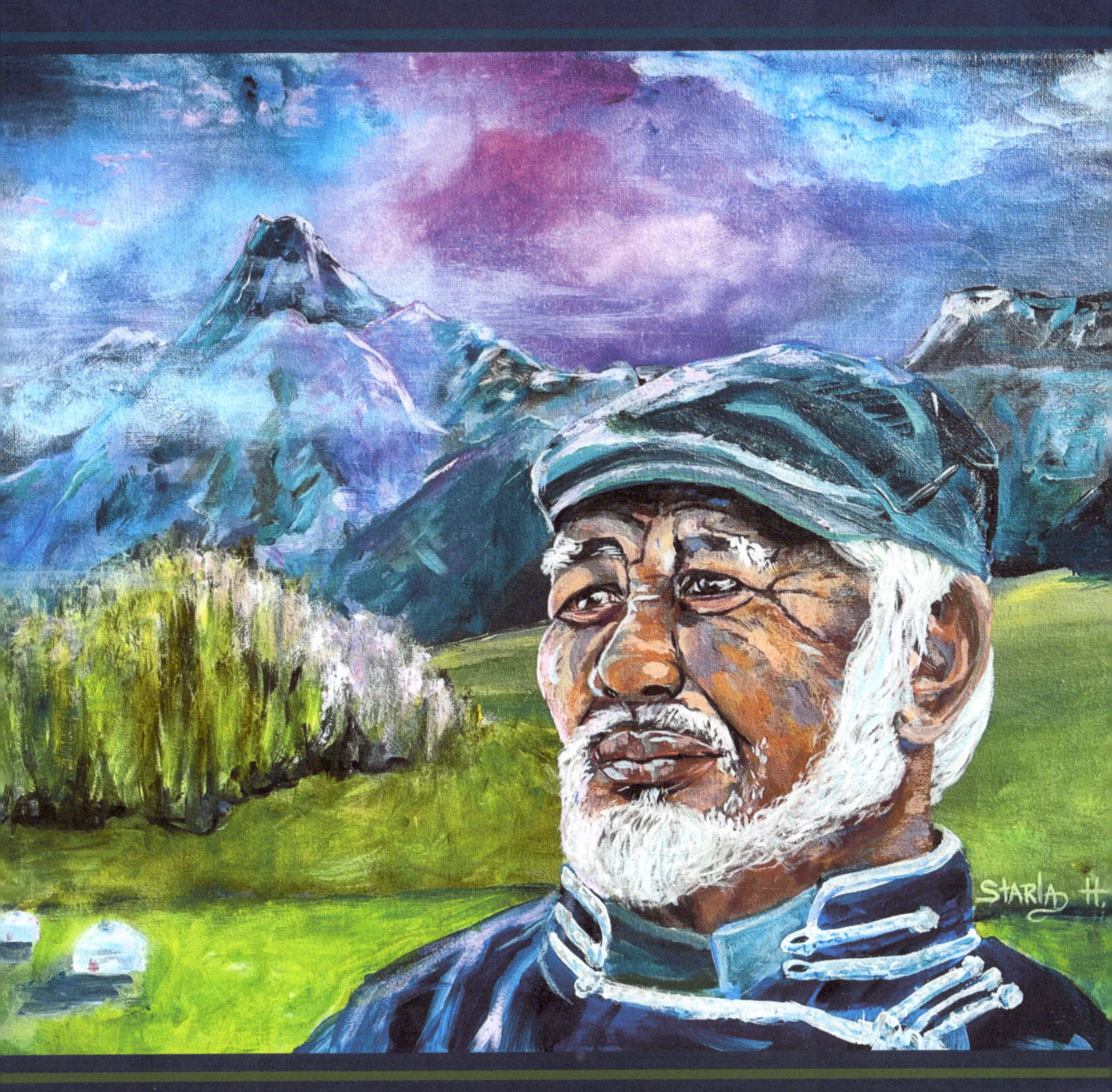

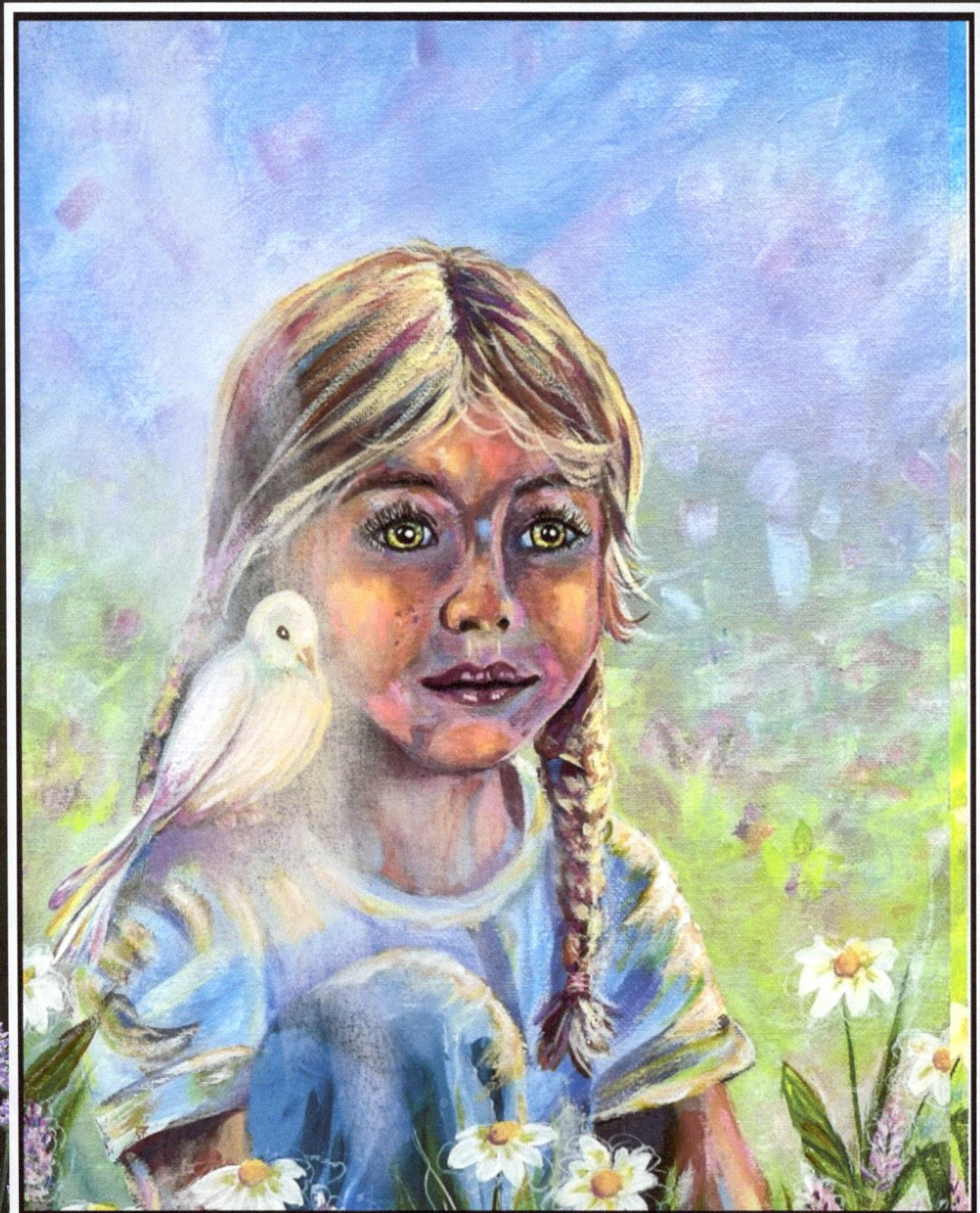

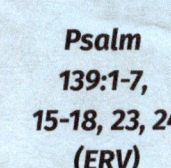

Psalm 139:1-7, 15-18, 23, 24 (ERV)

Lord, you have tested me,
so you know all about me.

You know when I sit down and when I get up.
You know my thoughts from far away.
You know where I go and where I lie down.
You know everything I do.
Lord, you know what I want to say,
even before the words leave my mouth.

You are all around me—in front of me and behind me.
I feel your hand on my shoulder.

I am amazed at what you know;
it is too much for me to understand.
Your Spirit is everywhere I go.
I cannot escape your presence.

You could see my bones grow as my body took shape,
hidden in my mother's womb.
You could see my body grow each passing day.
You listed all my parts, and not one of them was missing.

Your thoughts are beyond my understanding.
They cannot be measured!
If I could count them, they would be more than all the grains of sand.
But when I finished, I would have just begun.

God, examine me and know my mind.
Test me and know all my worries.
Make sure that I am not going the wrong way.
Lead me on the path that has always been right.

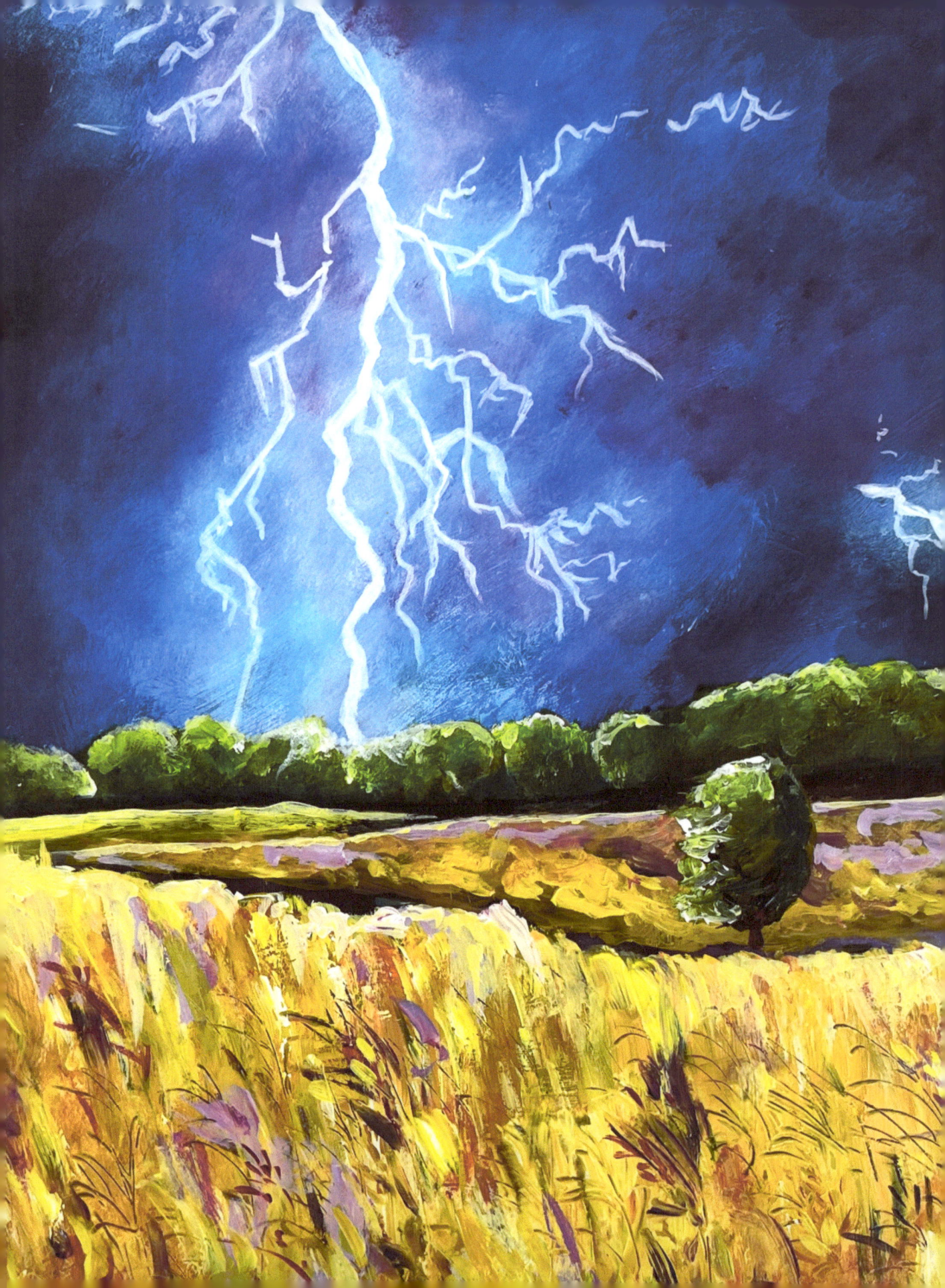

Psalm 144:1-7a,12-15 (ERV)

Praise the Lord! He is my Rock.
He prepares me for war.
He trains me for battle.

He loves me and protects me.
He is my safe place high on the mountain.
He rescues me. He is my shield.
I trust in him. He helps me rule my people.

Lord, why are people important to you?
Why do you even notice us?

Our life is like a puff of air. It is like a passing shadow.

Lord, tear open the skies and come down.
Touch the mountains, and smoke will rise from them.

Send the lightning and make my enemies run away.
Shoot your "arrows" and make them run away.
Reach down from heaven and save me!

May our sons be as strong as trees
and our daughters as beautiful as the carved columns of a palace.
May our barns be filled with crops of all kinds.
May our sheep produce so many lambs,
that thousands of sheep will fill our fields.

And may our cows be heavy with calves.
May no enemy break through our walls
or carry away any of our people.
May there be no cries of pain in our streets.

How wonderful to have such blessings!
Yes, great blessings belong to those
who have the Lord as their God.

Psalm 107:8, 9 (NLT)

Let them praise the Lord for his great love
and for the wonderful things he has done for them.

For he satisfies the thirsty
and fills the hungry with good things.
Psalm 107:8,9 (NLT)

How much you have done, Adonai my God!
Your wonders and your thoughts toward us —
none can compare with you!
I would proclaim them, I would speak about them;
but there's too much to tell!   Psalm 40:5 (CJB)

The young lions lack [food] and grow hungry,
But they who seek the Lord will not lack any good thing.
Psalm 34:10 (AMP)

He redeems your life from the Pit;
he crowns you
with faithful love and compassion.
He satisfies you with good things;
your youth is renewed like the eagle.
Psalm 103:4,5 (CSB)

Faithful Love Compassion

The Lord will always lead you.
He will meet the needs of your soul in the dry times
and give strength to your body.
You will be like a garden that has enough water,
like a well of water that never dries up.
Isaiah 58:11 (NLV)

"Blessed [joyful, nourished by God's goodness]
are those who hunger and thirst for righteousness
[those who actively seek right standing with God],
for they will be[completely] satisfied.
Matt. 5:6 (AMP)

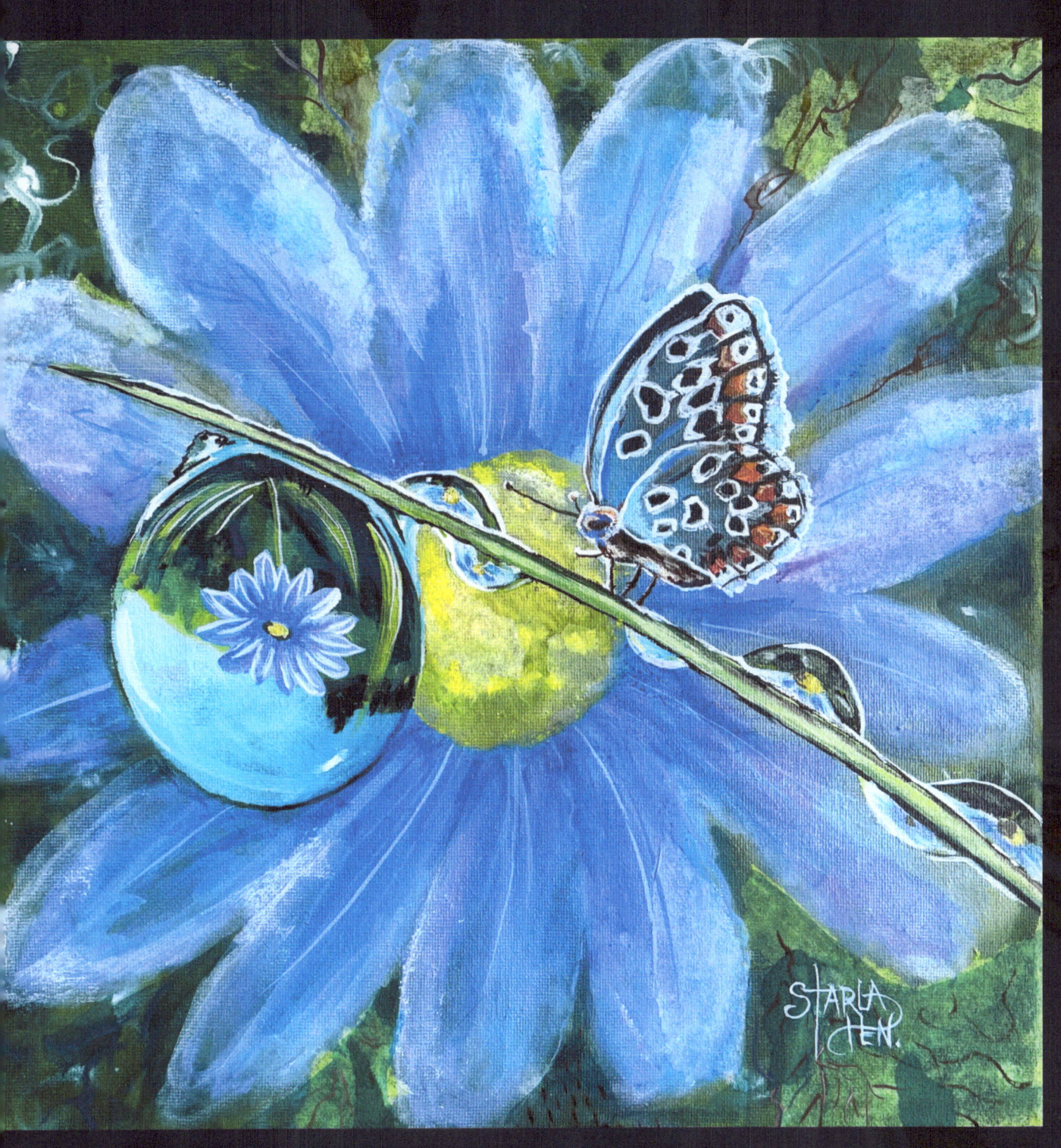

Psalm 16:11 (CJB)

**You make me know the path of life;
in your presence is unbounded joy,
in your right hand eternal delight.**

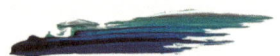

You feed them from the abundance of your own house,
letting them drink from your river of delights.
For you are the fountain of life,
the light by which we see. Psalm 36:8, 9 (NLT)

Now this is eternal life: that they may know You,
the only true [supreme and sovereign] God,
and [in the same manner know]
Jesus [as the] Christ whom You have sent. John 17:3 (AMP)

and the ransomed of the Lord will return
and come to Zion with singing, crowned with unending joy.
Joy and gladness will overtake them,
and sorrow and sighing will flee. Isaiah 35:10 (CSB)

But as the Scriptures say,
"No one has ever seen,
no one has ever heard,
no one has ever imagined
what God has prepared for those who love him."
I Corinthians 2:9 (ERV)

Surely goodness and mercy and unfailing love
shall follow me all the days of my life,
And I shall dwell forever [throughout all my days
in the house and in the presence of the Lord.
Psalm 23:6 (AMP)

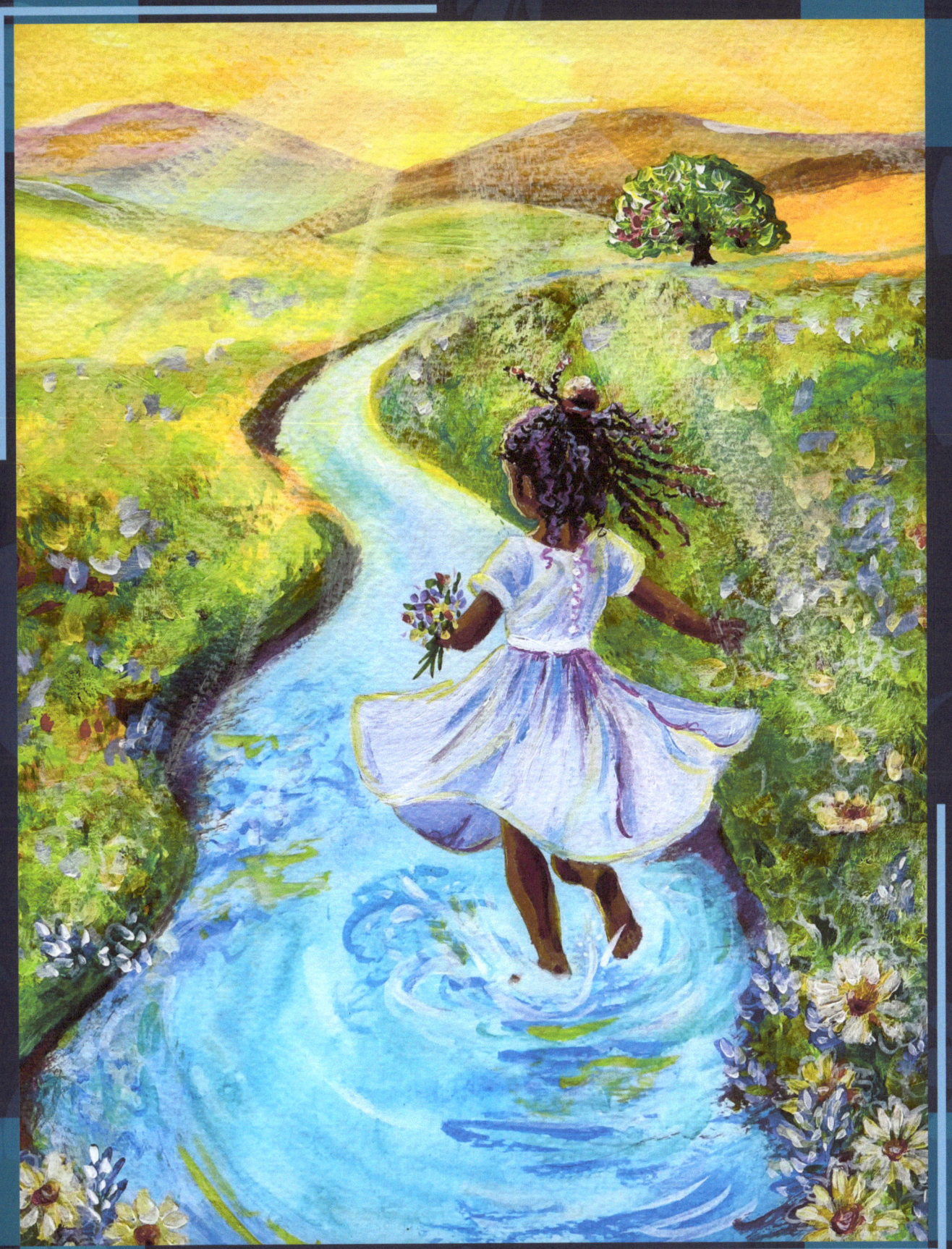

Artist's Notes

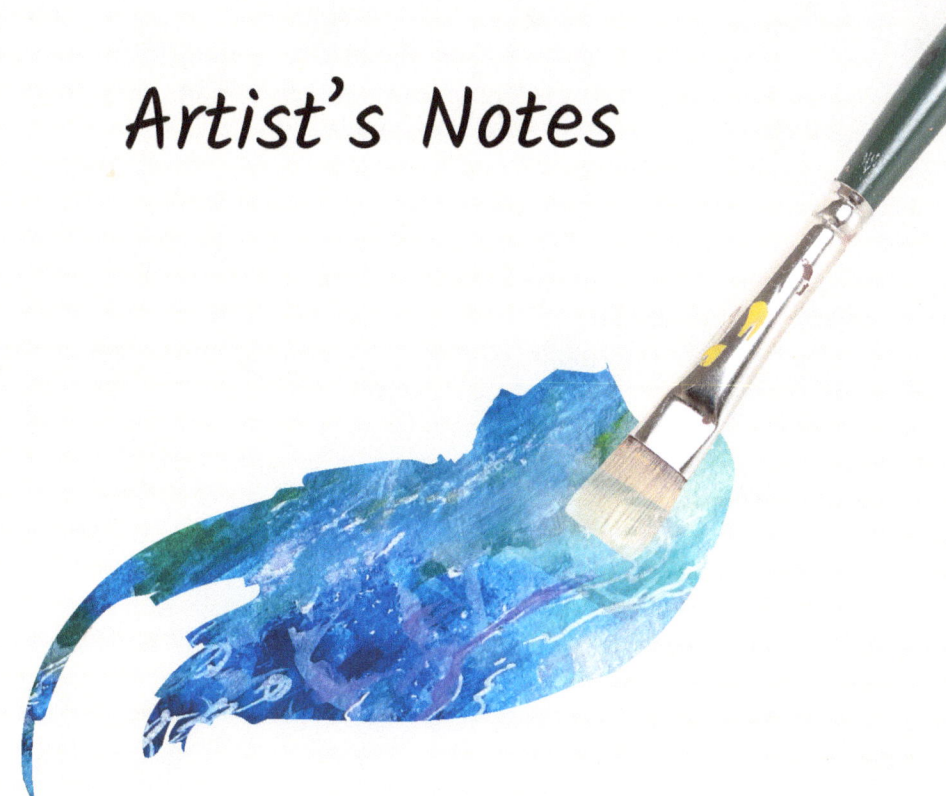

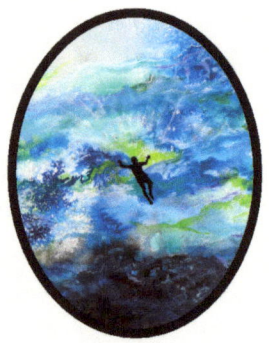

How do you paint a person drowning under water, hopeless in their situation? I wasn't sure, but put down a lot of acrylic inks, sprayed them with water, and this is the result The verses talk about how the waters even threaten one's life. In the middle of our despair, sometimes all we can get out is "Help, God!" or "Why?" And that's ok. Be real with Him. He can handle your emotions.

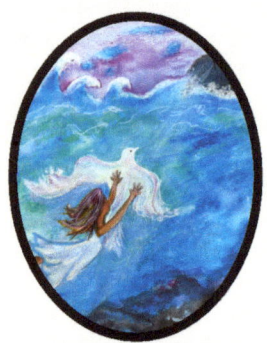

I wanted to paint hope in the midst of desperation. The dove represents the Holy Spirit, who is our Helper, pointing us to Jesus. He is present in the thick of trouble, even though we may not feel Him or be aware of Him. As we cry for help, there is mercy and love at the cross. Only Jesus can truly redeem a situation.

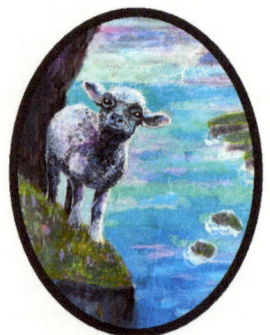

This little lamb is in trouble. Whether by disobedience, or circumstances beyond it's control, it knows enough to call out for help! Sometimes there are no words in grief, just tears. He bends down and hears our weeping.. He knows everything about our situation and His heart is moved with compassion.

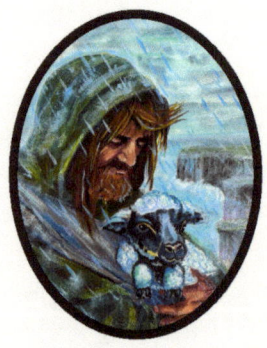

Can you imagine a sheep stranded on the Dover cliffs of the UK? This shepherd has gone through pouring rain, perhaps a lightning storm or braving a mud slide, maybe even needing to descend down a steep cliff to rescue His sheep. Our Shepherd is loving, compassionate, and strong. He knows your situation completely. Rescued, this lamb's panicked breathing starts to calm as it is held close to the Shepherd's heart, listening to his soothing voice. Just be held.

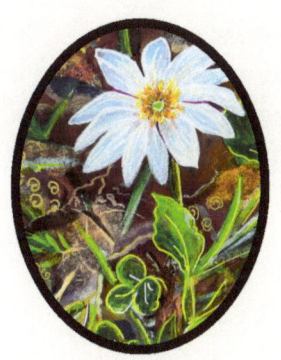

Sometimes pain in our hearts can be caused by choosing our selfish ways instead of listening to God. When sin is entertained in our hearts, the Lord will not hear us. David's prayer in Psalm 51 was written after being confronted about lusting, committing sexual sin, and murdering. Yet, God calls David a man after His own heart. God will not despise a broken and humble heart. Like a white flower on the dead forest floor, God will cleanse, revive, and make new.

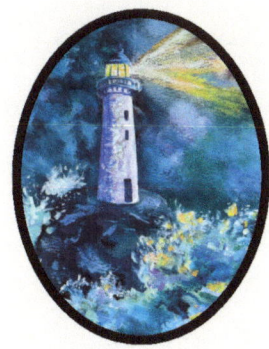

I grew up not far from where the mouth of the Columbia River meets the mighty Pacific. When the currents collide, there can be massive waves and dangerous stormy waters for anyone trying to navigate through. A lighthouse is crucial to survive through rough waters. Jesus Christ, our Lighthouse, calms our raging hearts; leading us to safety.

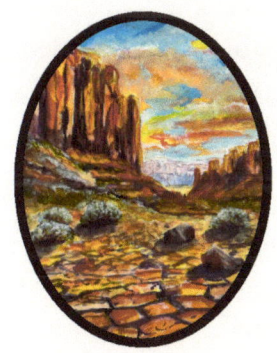

Experiencing a summer cutting firewood with my dad in the high mesas of Colorado, I know a little of the dryness and heat of a desert. Years later, in the Western Colorado desert bordering Utah, I came close to heat stroke. When your entire body craves water, you are very aware of its life giving power. This all encompassing thirst is what I tried to portray here; with absolutely no water in sight - thirsting for the living God. Only He can meet our deepest needs.

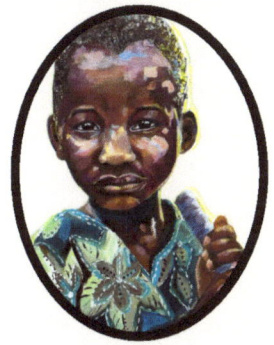

Most of us have a hard time relating with how thirsty a deer might be for water. However, we can imagine how thirsty a child in the African desert might be. We can imagine how his tongue must feel like sandpaper in the blazing scorching sun. As much as this child needs water, does our inner self thirst for God? Spiritual dryness is only quenched by drinking from the One who offers us living water that will never run dry.

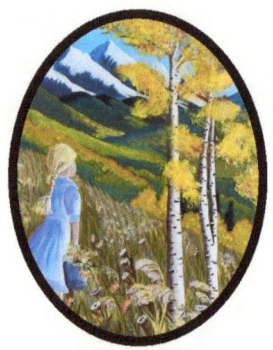

 A most memorable and breathtaking time was standing with my father in the midst of an aspen grove high in the mountains of Colorado. Hearing the breeze rustle the leaves and looking across the vast expanse into majestic beauty caused me to just stop - stop speaking, stop moving, and just be still. The awesome Creator is never caught by surprise by your circumstances. He is fully aware of your situation. Quiet your heart; know that He is God.

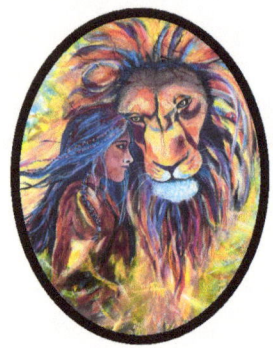

Have you ever read the *Narnia* books by C.S Lewis? Even as a child, the stories were ingrained into my heart. The title of this book, "Into the Lion's Mane" refers to abiding in the presence of Jesus Christ, the Lion of Judah. When He acts, who can stand in His way? When He speaks, "Be still!", the silence is deafening. When He pours out His love, His presence is overwhelming. His love gives us the strength to carry on. There is no Refuge like our God!

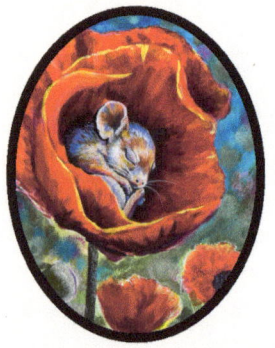

So many different subject matters went through my mind as possibilities to illustrate this particular verse. However, once the idea of a whimsical mouse tucked in a poppy came, I could not shake it. Poppies remind me of our veterans. So many veterans suffer with PTSD, and part of that is finding it difficult to sleep. In Jesus, there can be sweet rest and peace. God, our Provider, the Peace Giver, gives to His beloved ones, even in their sleep.

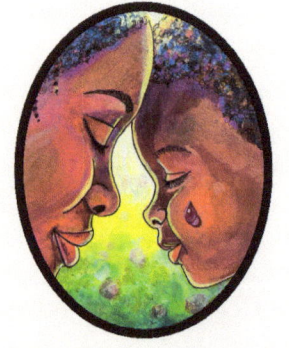

Just as a mother's gentle words console an upset child, so God comforts us through His Holy Spirit and His powerful Word. Hearing God's voice comforts roller coaster emotions, revives the exhausted, mends shattered hearts, and strengthens weary souls. Lord, make my heart receptive to Your quiet clear voice.

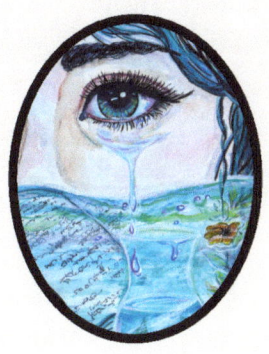

Sometimes our tears flow like a river. The Bible states that God collects our tears in a bottle. If there is a collection of tears to be had, His hands are near - so near as to be wiping those tears from our eyes - lovingly and gently collecting them. Each tear is recorded in His book. (Look closely at the small words on the book) The lonely tears, the silent tears, and the tears of the soul caught in the back of your throat, ready to burst from your heart; none go unnoticed by God. He is near, dear friend; nearer than you know.

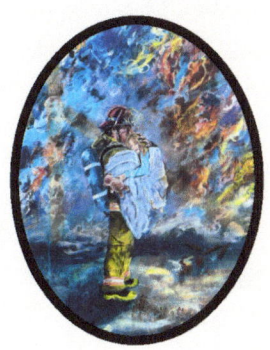

In the fall of 1986, most everything I owned was destroyed in a devastating, blazing fire. However, in the midst of it, God showed up; demonstrating His deep love to me - His child. Owning tremendous wealth, cannot even compare to the priceless treasure of knowing Jesus Christ. Years after this fire, I was facing a different kind of fire - sudden back surgery or paralysis. Shocked, hopeless and terrified, this huge canvas painting was born. Are we trusting completely in our "Fireman", Jesus Christ? Fling yourself on the Savior to see you through, no matter the intensity of the flames.

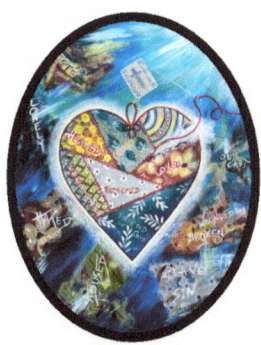

God is our Healer - the Healer of the brokenhearted. Often our wounds are not healed suddenly, but rather stitch by stitch. That's why there is a piece left on this patchwork heart still to be sewn. God is not finished with us yet. I used red thread to represent the blood of Jesus. The fabric pieces in the background represent our shattered broken lives. Only the Master Mender can truly bring beauty from ashes and joy from mourning.

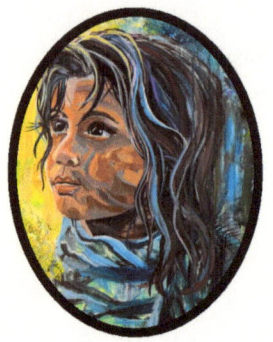

Longer ago I tried painting without blending all the brush strokes into smooth blends. Instead, I left the distinct strokes of the paint brush. In doing so, there was a piece of both pain and hope captured in this piece. There is no pain so deep that the love of God cannot redeem.

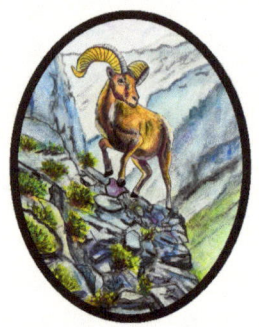

As a teenager, there were many trips through the Canadian Rockies. Sometimes, we would see these beautiful creatures. Look carefully under one of this bighorn sheep's front feet. There is a rock in the shape of a heart to represent God's love that keeps us from stumbling and falling. Only His love is true and stable, keeping us grounded.

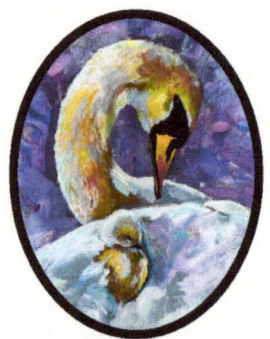

Have you ever watched how a bird is so protective of its young? God protects us in such a way! He is near enough for His shadow to fall over us. He is watching and mindful of our pain.
(This painting reminds me of my mother. She loved swans and passed of leukemia)

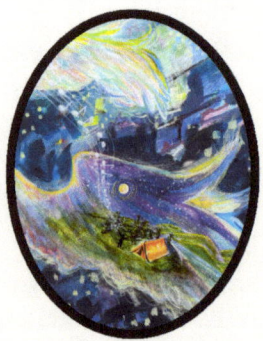

God is light and in Him is no darkness at all. There is no shadow in light. A candle flame does not cast a shadow on the wall. How do you portray perfect light? You can't really, but wanted to try to show in some pictoral way that we as children of God are completely under His watchful, powerful, loving care. As we live under His shadow we can be assured He knows everything we are experiencing.

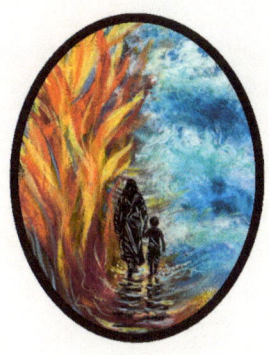

Sometimes the journey through trauma and sorrow can feel as if we are walking through a torrential flood or a devastating fire. The promise is that our Savior holds our hands, and walks with us. His voice speaks, "Fear Not! I am with you." We are not alone. HIs presence carries us and is healing solace to our souls.

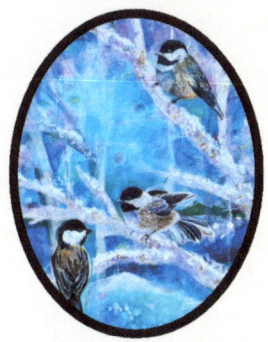

In 1986, shortly after my possessions went up in flames, I felt so alone, useless, overweight, and ugly. That winter day while watching some birds on a feeder, God reminded me that He not only cares for the perfect looking ones, but also for the straggly and fat ones. There is not one bird He does not know. My friend, you are of much more value than the birds! Your Heavenly Father cares, sees, and provides!

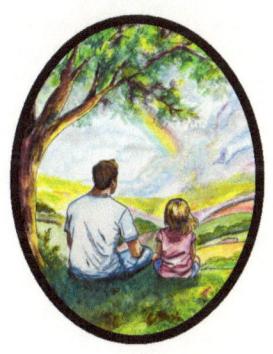

This painting shows a child with her loving, gentle dad. As a good father loves to show his children favorite places and tell them all about natural wonders in nature, is not our Heavenly Father delighted when we want to be with Him? Drawing close to Him, His wonders are shown, revealing light on some of His secrets. As a child, there was a plaque on the wall seen each day. "Call to me and I will answer you and tell you great and incomprehensible things you do not know." Jeremiah 33:3 (CSB).

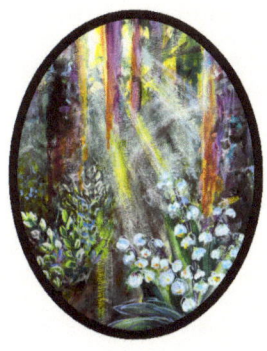

Lily of the valley flowers are in the foreground, representing the faithful love of Jesus. LIght streaming through the forest was painted to show the presence and strength of the Lord in every situation - pointing our floundering heart and wandering feet in the right direction. He is with us, even in the lonely dark unknown.

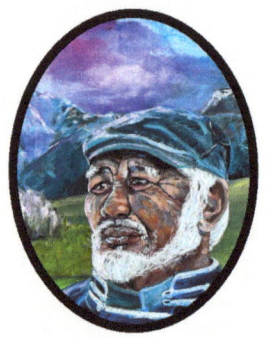

This painting portrays a real person and mountain range in Mongolia. While living there from 1994-'99, I often passed through these majestic mountains and took photos as we stopped and filled our senses with the vast stillness. Living in a small remote village, the Lord's protection was very evident and His guidance was given. Space, time and purpose of this book do not allow for the telling of some amazing stories, but this Psalm reminds me of God's faithfulness in protecting and leading. More recently, a professional photographer (Bayayr Balgantseren) gave the liberty to use one of his amazing portraits as a reference photo for the person in the foreground. In your difficult lonely places, you can truly trust Him. He is your strong loving Heavenly Father.

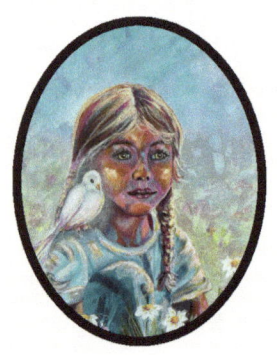

Tears were often close to the surface while painting this portrait. She reminded me of myself. Alone, in a cold dark gym at five years of age, I asked Jesus to be my Savior. From that moment on, the Holy Spirit (represented by this dove) took up residence in my life. The dove is at rest - completely at home. The presence of the Holy Spirit in the lives of His children is beautiful. He is with you and is aware of your circumstances dear friend, no matter what you are walking through.

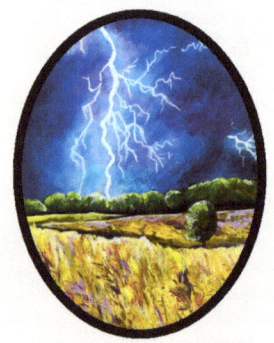

This painting, coupled with Psalm 144, demonstrates God's power. The One who sends lightning at His command is also the One who teaches how to live and how to find our strength. He is the One who prepares us for trials and is our Refuge as we walk through them. He is the Giver of every blessing, represented by the wheat. Ask God for eyes to recognize His powerful loving hand in your situation -no matter how difficult.

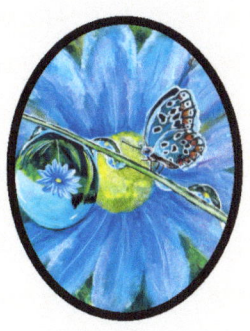

Have you heard of "macro photography"? In this painting I wanted to capture a glimpse of the intricate world of what raindrops mean to tiny creatures. Do you see the blue flowers reflected in the water droplets hanging from a blade of grass? A common everyday butterfly is drinking its sustenance for the day and all around it sees the handiwork of God mirrored many times over in tiny spheres. My friend, God cares for you deeply. He knows what you need, both for your life physically as well as for your thirsty heart. Even in pain, He provides beauty. The Giver and Sustainer of life will certainly take care of you. Choose to trust Him.

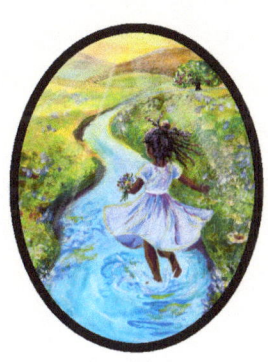

Heaven! God doesn't tell us everything there is to know about heaven. My guess is that there wouldn't be enough pages to write about it all. We do understand enough to know that it will be beautiful, wondrous, and wildly beyond all that we could ever imagine or think. In this painting, I tried to express an inkling of the joy we might feel when we enter heaven's doors. All sorrow, suffering, pain will be wiped away with one glimpse of Jesus' face - only complete joy in His presence.

How can I know Jesus?

Salvation is simple enough
for a child to understand.

The following pages include splashes of color with
verses to help point you to
coming into faith and relationship
with the only living true God.

A simple way to explain is through colors
first introduced as the wordless book by
Charles Spurgeon in 1866.

I came to know the Lord while yet a young girl
and as a visual learner, the wordless book
was easy to remember and understand
through the aid of simple colors.

Prayerfully ask God to give you understanding
as you read through these verses
and pour out your heart to Him in response.
He hears you.

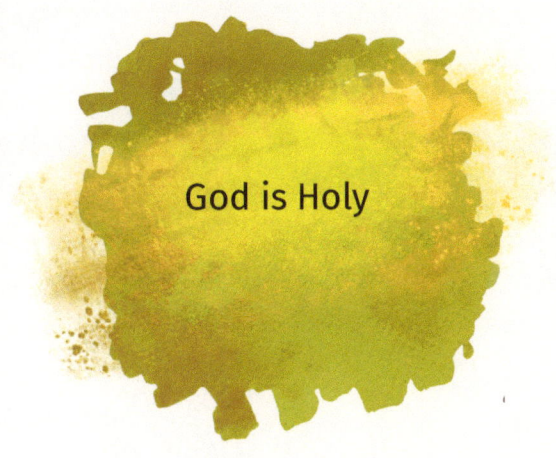
God is Holy

This is the message we have heard from him and declare to you: God is light, and there is absolutely no darkness in him. I John 1:5 (CSB)

Anyone whose life is not holy will never see the Lord. Heb. 12:14b (ERV)

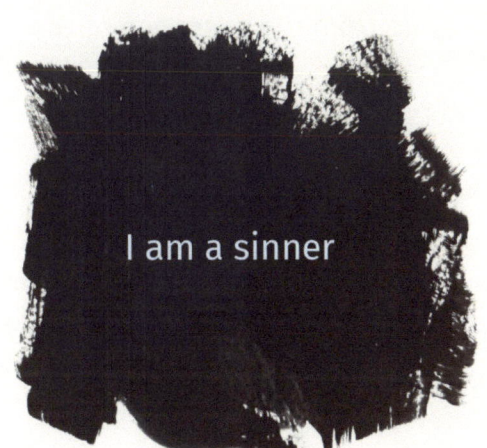
I am a sinner

For everyone has sinned; we all fall short of God's glorious standard. Romans 3:23 (NLT)

The human heart is the most deceitful of all things, and desperately wicked.
Who really knows how bad it is? Jer. 17:9 (NLT)

You get what is coming to you when you sin. It is death! But God's free gift is life that lasts forever. It is given to us by our Lord Jesus Christ. Romans 6:23 (NLV)

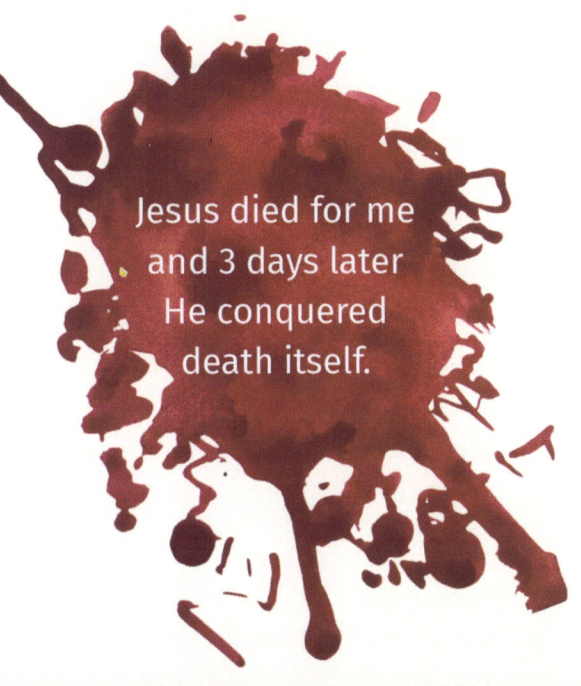
Jesus died for me and 3 days later He conquered death itself.

The law says that almost everything must be made clean by blood. Sins cannot be forgiven without a blood sacrifice. Heb. 9:22 (ERV)

But God clearly shows and proves His own love for us, by the fact that while we were still sinners, Christ died for us.
Romans 5:8 (AMP)

But God raised Him from the dead; and for many days He appeared to those who came up with Him from Galilee to Jerusalem, Acts 13:30, 31a (NASB)

...the blood sacrifice of Jesus, God's Son, washes away every sin and makes us clean.
But if we confess our sins, God will forgive us. We can trust God to do this. He always does what is right. He will make us clean from all the wrong things we have done.
I John 1:7b, 9 (ERV)

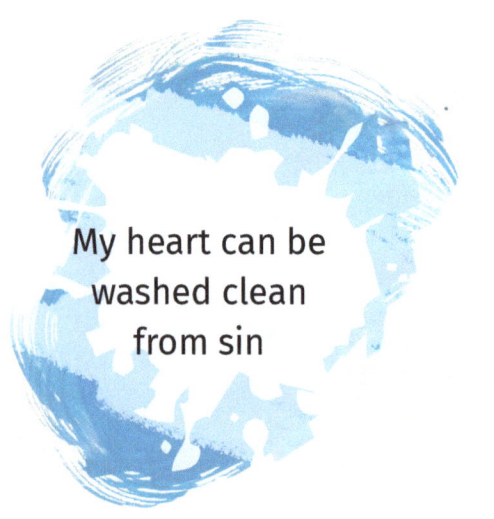

My heart can be washed clean from sin

Therefore repent and return, so that your sins may be wiped away, in order that times of refreshing may come from the presence of the Lord;
Acts 3:19 (NASB)

God saved you by his grace when you believed. And you can't take credit for this; it is a gift from God. Salvation is not a reward for the good things we have done, so none of us can boast about it.
Ephesians 2:8,9 (NLT)

But to all who believed him and accepted him, he gave the right to become children of God.
John 1:12 (NLT)

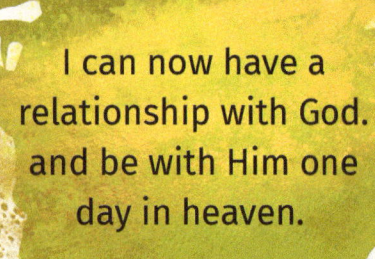

I can now have a relationship with God. and be with Him one day in heaven.

"For God so loved the world that he gave his only and unique Son, so that everyone who trusts in him may have eternal life, instead of being utterly destroyed. John 3:16 (CJB)

Therefore, if anyone is in Christ, he is a new creation; the old has passed away, and see, the new has come. 2 Cor. 5:17 (NASB)

Not vital for salvation, but after one trusts in Jesus for salvation, there are some basics for spiritual growth.

Like a plant needs basic elements to properly develop, so spiritual **GROWTH** happens as we are nurtured in our faith.

The Holy Spirit lives in you.
Read the Word and do it.
Talk to your Heavenly Father.
Meet with other believers.

The truth is the Good News. When you heard the truth, you put your trust in Christ. Then God marked you by giving you His Holy Spirit as a promise.

The Holy Spirit was given to us as a promise that we will receive everything God has for us. God's Spirit will be with us until God finishes His work of making us complete. God does this to show His shining-greatness.
Eph. 1:13, 14 (NLV)

Like newborn babies, long for the pure milk of the word, so that by it you may grow in respect to salvation, if you have tasted the kindness of the Lord.
I Peter 2:2,3 (NASB)

Your word is like a lamp that guides my steps,
a light that shows the path I should take. Psalm 119:105 (ERV)

Do not worry. Learn to pray about everything.
Give thanks to God as you ask Him for what you need. Phil. 4:6 (NLV)

Let us help each other to love others and to do good.
Let us not stay away from church meetings. Some people are doing this all the time.
Comfort each other as you see the day of His return coming near.
Hebrews 10:24, 25 (NLV)

About the Artist

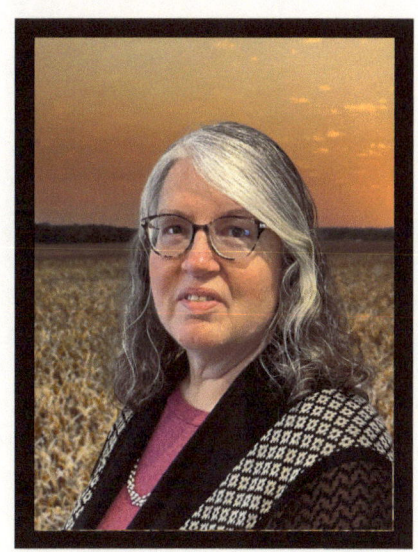

Starla Henninger, a self-taught artist, grew up in the Pacific Northwest. She is a Prairie Bible College graduate, being involved in cross-cultural missions in northern Canada, Mongolia, and Cambodia for 11 years. While in Mongolia, she met her husband, Tom, and has been married for over 25 years with three young adult children residing in Oklahoma City.

After the birth of their first child, Starla began exploring the world of painting. What began as simply painting botanicals and illustrating personal Bibles has grown into vibrant artwork incorporating a variety of artist mediums. Fresh perspectives in word pictures found throughout Scripture are hand painted to life in bold colors. As you observe the artwork, may your heart be pointed to the Master Artist Himself, the Creator of all things beautiful.